Blogging Your Way To Riches

Emma Bradley and Lynn James

Published by Emma Bradley and Lynn James

Copyright © Emma Bradley and Lynn James

First published in the United Kingdom in 2016 by Emma Bradley and Lynn James.

For more information for to www.bloggingyourwaytoriches.com.

Acknowledgements

Where do you start with acknowledgements when so many people have inspired you over the years and months leading up to writing your first book?

When we set ourselves the challenge of writing and self-publishing our first book within three months of meeting many would doubt it could be achieved, but we have done it. Along the way we have received fantastic support from the blogging community and many in our personal lives.

We want to pay special thanks to a few amazing people for their encouragement, belief and support as they helped us achieve our dream.

Hannah Fleming (Hi Baby Blog) met some crazy deadlines in getting our Blogging Your Way To Riches website live. She is a digital whizz and we thank her for her patience and inspired design work.

Di Coke (Super Lucky Me) and Tom Church (Latest Deals) were both generous with their time and knowledge, giving amazing insider tips on writing and self-publishing a book. Without them, we imagine we could have made many mistakes.

+

Emma Barnfield Photography are responsible for the fantastic photos used on both the book cover and the Blogging Your Way To Riches website. Thank you for seeing our vision and editing us to look fabulous!

Emma Wright for proof reading our book with another crazy deadline and for giving the very first honest and detailed critique. Thank you to the group of selected people who reviewed the book before 'print' was pressed. Thank you to Becky Goddard Hill, Cathy Whitmore, Emma Conway, Tom Church, Faith Archer and Debbie Smith.

Personally, Lynn would like to say the hugest thank you to her husband Vinny and boys Dylan, Josh and Jack who support her 100% with patience, time and love. Her troop of friends particularly Rebecca Megson and Anita Muir who have been there every step of the way from birth to book. Lynn's parents will be looking down and will be so proud of this huge achievement.

Emma would like thank her husband Lee and children Chloe, Dylan and Erin for their never-ending support. Also my parents for always believing in me and encouraging me to follow my dreams. Finally, to those who have always been there especially Faye Jones, the best friend a girl can have.

+

Contents

Chapter 1 - Introduction

Blogging can change your life. Do you dream of a flexible career where you choose your hours? A job that works around a growing family? If so blogging could be the answer for you.

Emma and Lynn are no longer wage slaves. Instead they choose the campaigns they want to participate in, they have achieved that elusive work life balance and they love what they do. Even better, they control their own destiny and have the opportunity to grow their dream business beyond all expectations.

This book has been written to give you the formula you need to turn your blog into a profit-making business. Whether you have just started blogging or mastered the basics this book is the tool you need to ensure you are moving towards success. Whether you want to make more money, be invited to blogging events or review everything from holidays to days out Emma and Lynn will help you set and achieve your goals.

Blogging Your Way To Riches will take you on a blogging journey and will give you the essential tips and advice for success. Furthermore, Emma and Lynn will share many of their achievements and just as important, the mistakes that they made in the early days. Each chapter will equip you with the information to build an online business.

They start with the skills of a blogger, what equipment is needed to start a blog and what your blog could look like. It then progresses into goal setting plus how to work with PRs and brands. Further chapters include making lots of money from your blog, why you should work collaboratively and unlocking the secrets to search engine optimisation (SEO). Finally, they talk about prolonging the future of your blog through diversification and networking and this is where your blog becomes a viable commercial business.

Emma and Lynn met at a blogging event where they connected and immediately saw similarities between themselves both professionally and personally. The very next day they decided to write a book together. What happened next is nothing short of fiction. Within three months they had met, written and self-published a book. Their desire to get this information out there drove them to push each other hard to write and finish the book in such a short space of time.

Together they came up with chapters and wrote them, checking in with each other daily. The writing of the book was completed in just four weeks. The reason they could write like this is because they know and understand blogging. Both Emma and Lynn had all the information and tips, it was just a case of getting it onto paper.

Emma and Lynn come from different backgrounds; Emma from teaching and Lynn is an accountant. This has given them different strengths when building their blogs but the combination makes them a blogging powerhouse. Despite the differences, they are both mums of three children, both have left professional careers and both started blogging on maternity leave with their third child.

Most importantly they have both established successful blogs and they also want you to experience the riches blogging can provide. They wanted to share their stories and help you reach your goals and dreams. Therefore, 'Blogging Your Way To Riches' was written to give you the confidence, skills and belief in your blog, that leads to unlimited success.

Emma's Story

Emma is married to Lee and together they have two girls and a boy, Chloe, Dylan and Erin. Emma graduated with a Social Policy degree and in 2003 qualified as a secondary school teacher teaching English. After several years in the classroom Emma was feeling disillusioned with the workload and she wanted a change of focus.

Emma's blog called 'Emma and 3' was conceived from her sick bed when on maternity leave with her third child Erin in 2009. Emma had been signed off work and she started to blog on a whim. There was no forethought, no grand plan; just an average mum with a passion for writing who was bored.

The blog became a hobby and an outlet. When Emma started blogging no-one really knew what a blog was and social influence was just beginning to creep across the internet. Even Emma's husband thought it was a passing fad.

However, the landscape was changing on a monthly basis and soon enough brands started approaching bloggers and inviting them to review their products. It was a very slow start and approaches were few and far between but it was fun.

In time they were being sent toys or clothes to review, which is a lovely perk of blogging. The children also enjoyed receiving things in the post to test out for their Mum's blog. It was probably a year or so into blogging that Emma was first paid to write a sponsored post. At this time a couple of really smart women set up the blogger networks, Tots100 and Britmums which helped to raise the profile of bloggers in the UK and blogging generally.

When Emma's daughter was almost two years old she was diagnosed with hip dysplasia. This rocked their world and suddenly Emma needed to take a sabbatical from teaching. Erin was about to undertake a year of treatment including seven trips to theatre where her hip would be operated on and pinned. During this time Emma used her blog to raise awareness and to also supplement her dwindling income. The blog was both an outlet for her feelings and also a new income stream in a time when she was not receiving wages.

In 2011 bloggers were earning around £50 a post and Emma thought this was pretty damn good! However, blogging escalated hugely during the year and bloggers became more in demand, mirroring what had already happened in America.

Emma started making more money and put as much effort into blogging as she did her teaching. Then the scales tipped. She decided that she wanted to write as her main income and she had the belief that blogging could become her career. This transformation did not happen overnight and it was another two years before the dream became a reality but in those two years strategic planning was bubbling away in the background. At this stage Emma started a second website called 'Mums Savvy Savings' with the aim to earn money from the outset. Much had been learnt along the way and being entrepreneurial she quickly realised that having two blogs could double her opportunities and importantly her income.

Emma left teaching in 2014 and it was the best decision for the family and herself. Comparing earnings is not straight forward as when she was teaching as she also had child care costs both before and after school. She also spent £200 a month on diesel and now she doesn't have these outgoings. That said her income is now on a par with what she was earning from teaching. In the past few months Emma has exceeded her old salary, but remember, this is now seven years in the making. Blogging is not a quick fix and it certainly isn't easy but you can make a living from blogging and it is probably easier than ever right now. This is in part due to some of the old timers who are more than happy to share their tips and stories which is why this book has been written.

Emma has always been a writer and often wondered where she would be if she had taken journalism or writing as a degree rather than social policy. As a teen, Emma wrote diaries. Every night she would write her innermost thoughts and her dreams. She used it as therapy when things were tough and those diaries are all stored away in a box in the garage. They are the tormented words of youth but demonstrate even back then she needed that outlet.

As social media grew Emma embraced it all. As a self-proclaimed over sharer, it was somewhat inevitable that she would turn to blogging. Emma has learnt to self-moderate her blog posts, especially as the children have got older, but generally if she thinks it, she shares it on social media.

By embracing blogging Emma's life changed, and her children know that blogging has given them many opportunities and experiences that others do not get. Using Emma's daughter Erin's words "we are a little bit famous!" Well she would think that when she has been in the national news, had amazing holidays given to her including a week in Corsica with Mark Warner, a few days at Porta Ventura, several weeks in UK holiday parks and stays at five-star luxury hotels to name a few.

Blogging has changed Emma and her family's lives and it can change yours too if you work hard. As a teacher Emma was constantly under pressure, trying to juggle family life with marking and lesson planning. Now Emma works as and when she chooses by taking on the campaigns she wants and never has to miss an assembly or sports match again. There is no greater story than freeing yourself and rewriting your future based on what you really want.

Lynn's Story

Lynn is married to Vinny and they have three young boys, Dylan, Josh and Jack. She spent most of her adult life working for big companies in various finance roles. She left university back in 1999 with a mathematics degree and started her corporate life with a bank in the city, whilst studying for her accountancy exams. Finally, at the age of 24 she finished ten full on years of exams and education and qualified as a CIMA accountant.

She then spent her career until the age of 38 working for various big companies in roles such as a Commercial Manager for petrol and tobacco at Tesco to a Sales Manager for pay as you go phones at EE. She saw a company go into administration, at Threshers, and worked for a company at the highest pinnacle of success at Tesco. A brilliant varied career means she has learnt many invaluable business skills.

It never felt 100% right, Lynn would start a role and be enthusiastic for a few months, but then it would die down, and she would get bored. This went on for 16 years. Yes, 16 years. Being employed was the "right" thing to do.

Working for companies like Tesco or EE were the right companies to work for. And with the jobs came a salary that grew over the years and a lifestyle that grew with it. Lynn recognised that she became trapped by her material world of house, lifestyle, car and holidays. How could she ever leave a job that earned great money and kept her family living a comfortable life?

Having children changes your work/life balance, and this took her a few years to address. Lynn has had three maternity leaves and returned to work after ten months or so after each baby, normally for financial reasons. History repeated itself a few times before she finally realised that corporate life wasn't for her.

+

In the meantime, Lynn, had been beavering away at a blog started during her final maternity leave in 2013. She used to keep a diary during her pregnancy and sent long emails to a childhood friend about her deepest feelings, worries and stories. After Jack arrived her mind soon wandered. A third maternity leave is different to the first or even the second. She had time to think and needed something productive to do.

The blog Mrs Mummypenny was born not long after Jack. The blog continued after Lynn's return to work, but she was never able to invest a decent amount of time and focus. However, she always had faith that it was a brilliant idea that could make money and change her family's lives.

Combining three children and a full-time job is hard. The guilt got to Lynn, that she wasn't doing anything really well, neither parenting or working. Four days a week she was away from her boys for 12 hours a day, and there were often work trips too. It was stressful, so when the opportunity arose for redundancy Lynn grabbed it with both hands. She actively did all she could to get that redundancy, giving her the chance and the funds to pursue her dreams. With careful planning the redundancy package could carry the family and pay the mortgage for 18 months, while Lynn devoted herself to Mrs Mummypenny.

+

Lynn's blogging story is described later in chapter 4, detailing the first six to twelve months of her blogging journey As Lynn's blogging story is so recent its relevant to talk through the story as you may be able to follow the same guidance and methods described to create success.

Chapter 2 - Why Should You Blog?

Individuals blog for many different reasons and in this chapter, we are going to share some of the more popular reasons people start a blog. Making money from blogging is a relatively new phenomenon and even as little as seven years ago money was not considered a reason to start a blog. Yet today many savvy bloggers have set up blogs intending to make money as soon as possible. The various reasons for starting a blog include making memories and capturing childhood, which is why many new mums start blogs on maternity leave. Other bloggers intend to promote specific causes and campaigns. However, there are a growing number of people looking to make money from blogging. We will show you that not only can you make money but you can make a full-time wage, so whatever your goals are stick with Emma and Lynn to find out how you can change your life.

Online Journal

Just a few years ago many mums started a blog as an online journal. It is the modern equivalent to keeping a diary.

Today many of us live far from family and friends and a blog can be a great way to share what is happening in your life. Blogs allow you to send pictures across the globe and can help you feel connected to your family. This early start to blogging created the term 'mummy blogging' which has both positive and negative connotations.

Bloggers have had to fight some outdated stereotypes in the years since the national print media picked up on the mummy blogger tag but blogging has evolved since then. Blogging is certainly not restricted to mums or even to women. There are a growing number of male parenting bloggers making an impact proving the point that dads don't babysit, they parent!

The internet and free blogging platforms like Blogger and WordPress allowed people to start blogs to share stories and photos with the wider world. Anecdotally we have discovered that many bloggers kept diaries as a child and they see blogging as the modern equivalent. Blogs allow you to show others what you had done at the weekend. It keeps people up to date with your life no matter where you or they are. It is a bit like that yearly letter you receive in a Christmas card that informs you what a family has been up to for the last year. Blogging means you can do that on a more frequent basis.

+

Telling a story

Blogs cover all manner of niches in society from parenting, saving money, music, photography to everything in-between. Think of a topic and there will be a multitude of blogs out there being written and read on the subject. A new baby and maternity leave changes a family lifestyle immensely; it is a time of transition and it is no coincidence that many parenting blogs start at this stage.

Blogging can be a way of documenting childhood. For some women maternity leave is an isolating time and finding an online community can be a great support. Feeding a baby in the small hours of the morning may mean that mums are online more and sharing their new experiences. This can lead to the world of blogging and encourage other new parents to start telling their story.

One of our favourite parenting blogs is Mother's Always Right, written by Molly Forbes. Molly tells a tale in such a brilliant way and mixes just the right amount of humour, wit and carefully crafted parenting woes that you just nod your head in agreement. With the rise of stay at home fathers we have witnessed the growth of male bloggers sharing their early days and years of parenting.

Providing a Creative Outlet

We can heap lots of pressure on ourselves in our nine-five jobs and blogging can be a great tool in providing a creative outlet. Emma had lots of pen pals as a child and liked writing. Therefore it was somewhat inevitable that she turned to blogging. Many blogs showcase an individual's skills for example those who enjoy cooking or baking may choose to blog about their meals and cakes. A Mummy Too written by Emily Leary has nailed helping everyday mums to get more creative in the kitchen. Blogging gives recognition and a platform to share those skills.

Many bloggers are talented photographers and use their blog to showcase their talents in the hope it will lead to further opportunities. A prime example is an amazing woman like Katie Kirby from Hurrah for Gin who got a book deal for the cartoons shared on her blog.

Blogging has led to many career changes. Writing prose or poetry, being serious or funny, we all find our style and our slice of the internet is where we can express ourselves however we choose. If you are creative and make products to sell, a blog is a good way to showcase those products and build yourself a community. It can be a way to engage with your customers and build your small business. Having a blog can elevate your success.

+

Promoting a campaign

A blog is an informative way to promote a cause or run a campaign. When you or your child has a health condition, it can feel lonely and isolating. As you learn more about the condition you may want to share your experience, inform others about treatment options and what equipment and resources have helped you cope. Such blogs may be written by an individual or by a group of bloggers who share a common cause.

Emma blogged throughout her youngest daughter's hip dysplasia, which allowed an insight into her treatment. Blogging can give you a voice to raise awareness and there are blogs covering all types of campaigns.

Another example is the talented writer behind NorthernMum. Jane Pettit, blogs about her daughters Type 1 diabetes and complex regional pain syndrome and the challenges the family face on a regular basis.

One of the most successful blogs that also provides a positive insight into their family life is Downs Side Up written by the remarkable Hayley Goleniowska. Hayley has received the accolade of multiple awards for her blog, which started as an insight into their daughter Natty having Downs Syndrome. It quickly became a source of inspiration and advice for other families in similar situations. Hayley has recently been very involved in the TV documentary 'A World Without Down's Syndrome'.

This highlights that from small acorns mighty oak trees have grown. A blog can have an impact on society in ways no one expected. It can be a great release to write a campaign type of blog and it is a valuable source of information for others going through the same things too. Think of these blogs like your personal encyclopedia on a topic!

Working from home

Two income families are the norm now. Our lifestyles often require dual incomes due to the growing consumer society we live in.

+

As we travel more with our families, buy more designer goods and invest financially in our children this comes at a greater cost. Larger mortgages, the rise of feminism and having greater financial aspirations mean that women need to bring in more money. However, once we have children we often feel that all too familiar mummy guilt. We may try to juggle everything to provide financially for our children but parenting gets in the way of the work commute and late meetings. Working from home on a self-employed basis is a squad goal for a growing army of mums, and who can blame them? Emma and Lynn want to show women that it doesn't have to be that way and you can get a better balance.

Emma's personal journey mirrors the experience described above. Her three children had several health issues and she often had to take them to hospital for consultant visits. They also picked up every bug going and she would get called to come and collect them from school. This experience is not unusual and is especially true during primary school years, when children's immune systems are not as strong.

+

Emma often felt that she was not there for her children and it was not fair on her colleagues who had to try and pick up the pieces. Emma loved teaching but it just didn't work with three children. Therefore, she decided that working from home would be the ideal solution for her family. Preparation to leave teaching began well before handing in her notice. Emma started a second blog to have another income stream.

The biggest advantage of working from home is the flexibility it offers. No more missed sports days or assemblies. However, it comes at a price too, as you lose a regular salary and have to pitch for work opportunities in an ever-competitive space. Now that her children are all in full time education, Emma does not have any childcare costs which means she requires less monthly income than when she was teaching.

Working from home cuts costs travel and lunch costs but it is a lifestyle change as well as a work change. When doing the maths to see if self-employment is a viable option, consider what your fixed financial outcomes are. This means consider the big bills and the mortgage costs. Will working from home work for you?

In this ground breaking book Emma and Lynn want women to see that they can change their job and change their lives. They will inspire you to make the change as they share the secrets that they have learnt so far on their blogging journey. It has never been a better time to make the change and become your own boss. You can blog your way to riches.

Making money

A growing number of women start a blog with the clear intention of making money and who can blame them. It really is the greatest job of all, giving women everywhere the freedom to set their own goals and their own hours. In this book, we will guide you through what Emma and Lynn have learnt on their personal blogging journeys. Both Emma and Lynn have turned their blogs into viable businesses, choosing to shun the corporate and education sector in exchange for working for themselves. There are many ways to make money from blogging which are explored throughout the book and especially in chapter 11.

In brief, making money comes mainly in the form of sponsored posts, advertising, brand partnerships and affiliate marketing. Brands realised the power wielded by blogs and have since looked to work with good bloggers in a variety of exciting and innovative ways. We believe this is a trend which will continue to grow.

A blog can also launch other paid work opportunities. It can lead to social media management, freelance writing opportunities, blogger outreach and PR work.

We can't wait to share the secrets of how to up your game and make money from blogging. Blogging Your Way To Riches will inspire you to make more money from blogging and give you the confidence and skills to earn more than you thought possible. It is not a get rich quick scheme and it will take time and effort but it can be done as we will demonstrate.

+

Bullet point the reasons you have started a blog. This will help you focus.

+

Chapter 3 - The Essential Skills Needed as a Blogger

Emma and Lynn have both been extremely fortunate to meet many bloggers from all different sectors and niches since they started blogging as a business. A great part of the blogging world involves meeting other bloggers at events, be that bigger events such as Blogfest, Britmums Live and the MAD blog awards or at smaller brand events. You will learn the required blogger skills from these events.

Fantastic events have been attended such as a bake-off challenge with Smart Energy GB, Finding Dory paper crafting with Epson & Disney and chocolate making with Tena. These not only give you a great experience doing something fun but you also get to meet the best bloggers in the business with fabulous blogging skills. Conversation and chat is perfect at these events, use them to glean insights and learn as much as possible. Now people search out Emma and Lynn at these events. This was one of the lightning bolt moments when they knew they had to write this book.

Here is our list of skills that we think every great blogger should aim for.

Be a great writer

The blogs that we return to time and time again are the ones written with passion and enthusiasm. They are the posts you read right until the end. These bloggers understand the craft and skill of writing. They know when to use a conjunction and an adjective. They know how to structure a post. They know how long a sentence or paragraph should be. They know to include headers and pictures making a post easier to read.

You must learn the craft of writing. A great place to go back to basics is homework with your children. Read lots of other brilliantly written blogs. What can you learn from them? How can you use a similar writing style? We all have our own particular style; it makes us unique but you can learn hints and tips from others.

Our favourite blogs for brilliant writing are Cash Carraway, the Comeback Mum and Amy Treasure. Cash the Comeback Mum is one of the most honest and fascinating blogs around. She has written about harrowing subjects from bankruptcy to domestic violence to losing her vagina.

Amy Treasure has an incredible knack to write from the heart on any subject, be that Coca Cola or domestic violence. She has a really special trait that makes us read many of her posts, even the sponsored ones. That is true influence.

Honesty, authenticity and passion

Emma and 3 was born as a blog to share Erin's health problems with the world. It was created from a desire to share the story with a captive audience. The blog posts and realities of dealing with a child's illness are hard-hitting and a truly authentic account of life's difficulties.

Authenticity is so important in blogging and pours out of a blog post if it's real. Alternatively, you can read through a sponsored post where the blogger isn't being 100% honest or has been paid to write a positive review of a product. We'll admit it, we have both done it. In the early days of Mrs Mummypenny Lynn wrote a couple of posts on subject areas that she wasn't completely comfortable with, to start earning some money. These posts are not as authentic as later posts where she stays true to her goals and morals.

+

Balance

Most blogs are born out of the desire to tell a story or to create an online diary. This is brilliant content for the early days of a blog. It helps attract early adopters who will promote and support you forever and a day. You need these people to stick with you!

By building an audience you can hopefully reach the right level of social followers and traffic and start to make money from your brand with sponsored posts.

Just remember your key aims and morals here and do not work with anyone and everyone who offers you money. Only work with brands that fit your site and your own brand. Balance out the real unpaid posts written from the heart with sponsored posts. Some bloggers have a self-imposed rule to only have one sponsored post a week and all other posts are not sponsored. Mix up your posts with funny stories or advice about the less fun bits of motherhood, or the more fun bits of parenting is a great way to engage with your readers.

+

Be a listener

It is a great idea to accept as many event invites as possible particularly in the early days - but then keep your mouth shut! Listen to those around you, ask questions, and pick the brains of other bloggers in your niche. You will hear a lot of stuff that you immediately object to and disregard, but you will also hear a few amazing gems.

Lynn remembers chatting to Aby from You Baby Me Mummy at Blogfest 2015, discussing the power of Instagram. Lynn didn't even know what Instagram was or how it worked until that point! So, from then on she worked her Instagram!

Aby also said that it was completely possible to earn £50,000 a year from blogging. Lynn latched onto this and it inspired her. It gave her the belief that with a lot of hard work she could get Mrs Mummypenny to work. Go with your gut and follow any guidance and advice that feels right.

+

Network

Later in the book, the whole of chapter 7 is dedicated to networking. We are firm believers in the power of networking, meeting people and the principle 'it's not what you know, it's who you know'. Go to events and launch parties. If you hear about an event, ask for a contact and get an invite. Brands will often pay travel expenses to these events so don't let the cost put you off, just ask if there is travel budget available.

Lynn attended Blogfest in November 2015 without knowing a soul. This would be a scary thing to do for most people, but she rocked up and made the most of an incredible event for newbie bloggers. She introduced herself confidently to people and made a beeline for the bloggers whose blogs she had been following. She ensured that she spoke to all the brands and attended the lectures that were most beneficial to her blog. She met many bloggers whom she has kept in touch with over the past year. It's great to build a list of bloggers on Twitter, as they can be really helpful for retweets.

We believe that we have both made our blogs so successful by being warm, friendly people in every event we attend. We have both got many commissions through chatting, introducing ourselves, getting to know others and telling people about our blogs. Go for it, get out of your comfort zone and get yourself to events where you can build your network and get work out of it.

There are also online networking groups you can join, particularly on Facebook. We recommend you join them. Search for groups that match your niche. Use these groups to ask questions. We have learnt things like search engine optimisation (SEO) tips and tricks to help you show up on Google search, advice on affiliate marketing to earn income, and how to sign up for Google AdSense advertising. However online activity is no substitute for face to face networking. Try to get along to as many events in person that you can.

Planning and organisation

To be a great blogger you need to master the art of planning and organisation. This is one skill where Lynn acknowledges that she needs to up her game.

If you want to blog your way to riches, you need to treat your blog as a business.

+

This includes setting your big goals, breaking those goals down into objectives and then making detailed to-do lists. Creating a business plan and cash flow forecasts will provide a brilliant long term view of your business. Your long-term plan should focus on just one or two big ticket goals. It's important to cement these as your main aims and objectives for business. Every job you take, or every piece of work you do should contribute towards these goals. Print out your goals and stick them up near where you work. Don't let anything detract you from your goals. Chapter 8 is dedicated to goal setting and helping you to plan your blog and business.

Then there are the short-term goals, which can include a weekly target, your everyday to-do list, a social media planner and a blog planner. Everything will help you be more effective and get more done in the same amount of time.

Get some great stationery or download and print out freebie printables and get planning.

Be prepared to get stuck in, learn and do lots yourself.

When you start a blog it's you on your own, learning and creating everything yourself. Sometimes you will make mistakes, but hopefully you will learn from them. But you must be prepared to get stuck in and learn as much as possible. Lynn spent her first six months learning like a sponge, mastering things like creating a blog on WordPress, and making plenty of mistakes along the way.

She experimented with plug-ins, set up her own hosting, tried to understand follow/unfollow links (to be explained later in the book), domain authority and search engine optimisation. She focussed on understanding the technicalities so that she could do most things herself. This meant that start-up costs of the business were very low.

You must invest in writing tons of brilliant content. Content really is king and is the thing that will make your website different to other blogs.

There are tons of admin tasks that you must get stuck in and do yourself. Your own books and accounts, setting yourself up as self-employed or a limited company. You need to organise everything yourself, from travelling to meetings to pitches.

You need to set up a separate bank account and keep track of money. You will need to chase debt, and face up to reality that sometimes you don't get paid. You will need to stay on top of paperwork. Remember the more you do yourself will lower your costs and therefore more profit will be made from your blog.

Be commercial

Do you want to make money from your blog? Of course you do, you wouldn't be here reading this book if you didn't! How much do you want to make from your blog? How are you going to earn that money? Just think of the financial freedom if you could blog to a place where it earns £1,000 per month, £2,000 per month or even £5,000 per month. If this is one of your big-ticket goals, then you have to look at your blog as a business with a commercial mindset.

The concept of being commercial is a simple one. It just means making as much money as possible, spending as little as possible and maximising your profit. Your profit can then be paid as wages.

When building your business run it as a tight ship. Do not spend money on things that won't give you a good return, only spend money on essentials. Lynn's start-up costs included a laptop, a tablet and a second-hand desk.

Think about your business expenses. Buy the cheapest train ticket for that meeting in London or better still ask the PR agency or client to cover the costs. Take packed lunches rather than buying food out and about. Don't buy coffee, bring it from home in a takeaway cup. There are little ways to save and it all adds up. Carry around a little note book where you can track your business expenses.

When growing your audience invest wisely in simple things like Facebook advertising. Facebook advertising is an effective and low priced way to increase your presence and likes. Some targeted Facebook advertising can work wonders. Focus on one or two social channels like Twitter or Instagram and work hard to increase the number of your followers

Diversification is also important. Don't put all your eggs in one basket and rely on all your income from a single source. Use a variety of methods to make money such as sponsored posts, affiliate income, testing new apps, product reviews and public speaking.

Professionalism

Professionalism is so important in the world of blogging and it stretches from your relationships with brands to PR agencies to other bloggers and service providers.

Professionalism will get you far, will make you memorable and trusted and will all lead to more work.

You may work directly with brands or with PR agencies. In both situations build a professional relationship which mainly means polite interaction. Stick to agreed objectives and timescales. If a brand asks you for a blog post on a specific day with a Facebook share and tweet on the same day, then stick to the deadline and deliver exactly what was agreed. Agree these things up front so there is no ambiguity.

Maintain these relationships by sending an email every couple of months with an updated media pack or a great post that they might enjoy.

There may be some professional services that you pay for, maybe logo design or an accountant. Always be professional with these service providers. These people make your life easier so look after them. If they help you and do a great job, then recommend them. You can also earn recommendation affiliate commission for this too.

Professionalism with other bloggers particularly in groups is so important. A reputation as a friendly and collaborative blogger will get you far. Both Emma and Lynn have had work passed on or shared due to their professionalism. They have been invited to events due to other bloggers recommending them to brands.

Collaborate with fellow bloggers and deliver what you said you would, when you said you would. If a blogger writes a post for your website, write one for theirs. Collaborate with other bloggers in the same niche as you.

There are lots of skills here that make up the perfect blogger. We hope you can relate to most of them or at least some of them. And if you think you can manage all of them, you have this blogging game nailed.

Be Thick-skinned

There is a slightly dark side to blogging that we must acknowledge and make you aware of. Beware of the internet trolls and haters. If you write about controversial subjects where there is likely to be a huge difference in opinion you may well get people disagreeing with you and telling you so. As your profile grows and you become more successful there will be people who might want to take you down.

+

Try not to focus on these unsavoury comments, who knows why the trolls do it, maybe to get a reaction? The best thing is not to rise to them. A second negative is comparing yourself to others and questioning why others have got jobs / campaigns when you have not. It is natural to feel a certain amount of jealousy. After all that can drive us to be competitive and to work harder not everyone can do every campaign. Be happy and positive for others, and karma will play its role. Let's make this blogging world a friendly one.

Chapter 4 - What to Expect in the First Six to Twelve Months of Blogging

We have covered the 'why you should blog' and 'the essential skills of a blogger'. Next we want to talk you through the first year of running a blog and the kind of things you can do to achieve success as quickly as possible.

This chapter is written by Lynn describing her first year as Mrs Mummypenny to the end of September 2016. From mistakes to successes, despair to celebrations Lynn tells it as it was.

The early days when I still worked full-time

Blogging was always a hobby for me which started during my third maternity leave with Jack. I set up a great basic blog and maintained it when I returned to work. I worked full time for EE for nearly 2 years before I took the risk and pursued the Mrs Mummypenny Empire.

My basic blogging model included setting up a self-hosted website and developing social media channels on Facebook and Twitter. I decided my blog name on day one and grabbed all the domain names and social accounts. I decided my blogging niche would be personal finance from the perspective of a mum of three.

I kept my blog updated with content and used to share a money saving tip on Facebook every day. I updated my website with new content every one to two weeks. One of my first website posts was 'Why I set up Mrs Mummypenny, my aims and ethos. Reading back it could be better, the language needs improvement, it's badly optimised for search engine traffic and it has grammar and spelling errors. However it is an interesting comparison for readers to see where I started and where I am now.

Mrs Mummypenny Ltd is born

All the stars were aligning, redundancy became an option and I left EE June 2015. The first thing I did was register for job seekers allowance. Being a personal finance expert I know that the moment you are made redundant you can claim for this benefit. Another sign was my job seekers advisor telling all about the government funded national enterprise allowance scheme. A scheme set up to help people like me into business with a bit of money (£65 per week for 13 weeks and then £33 per week for 13 weeks) to help get set up. I met with an advisor who tasked me with writing a business plan, cash flow forecast and survival budget. If these were signed off I was on the scheme.

This is the best thing to do in the early days of starting your business and should be the first thing you do to focus your mind.

"Failure to plan is planning to fail" – Benjamin Franklin

I set September 2015 as my trading commencement date. During the summer months, I sorted out all the admin tasks such as getting the company set up, opening a business bank account and planning the shareholder structure. I interviewed and appointed an accountant and got business cards printed.

I asked two EE contacts to assess and feedback on my business plan and financials plans, both had offered this support after I sent out my leaving email. Neither of them are involved in blogging but they are incredibly successful and have both owned small businesses since their early 20's. Their comments were so helpful and gave me new focus to succeed. One gave me three great pieces of advice for my first year of trading:-

1) Spend as little money as possible

2) Generate as much turnover as possible

3) Invest as much as you can afford in advertising.

+

The other questioned my belief and motives behind the business. Your heart, soul and mind has to be in the business 100% for it to work commercially and be a success. We now meet up maybe once a year and they are there if ever I need them for advice and guidance.

I wrote brilliant content as often as I could. I managed to publish twice a week up from once a week! All the social media channels were set up, from YouTube, Instagram and, Pinterest to, Snapchat and Google+ I worked on plans to significantly increase my likes on Facebook and followers on Twitter.

Engaging with Blogging Communities

I went out of my way to engage with communities and groups. The parent blogging community stood out as the one to help the most. I bought a ticket to Mumsnet Blogfest to meet people, talk to brands and get my name out there. I engaged with a few brands and started doing some freebie sponsored posts. My first job was with 'Up at the O2' and Wagamama's. I thought I was in heaven. I was given free tickets to climb the O2 and vouchers to pay for lunch for my hubby and me! We had a brilliant day out, doing something I would never normally do, followed by a free lunch.

I went to a Lean In networking event where I met my friends and collaborators Claire and Nicky Wacey of Wacey Style. We have since worked on various projects together. I went to Stylist Live and got busy handing out my business cards to every business going! I really took every opportunity I could to attend events where brands would be and where I could meet other brilliant collaborative minds.

Mumsnet Blogfest was a turning point both from an inspirational point of view and a knowledge point of view. I met so many other brilliant bloggers in person who I had read online. I attended several great seminars and talks on subjects like how to win at brand relationships and how to take great photos (I've not mastered that one yet!). I caught up with a couple of parenting/personal finance bloggers, one of whom told me about a UK Money Bloggers Facebook group.

I joined up as soon as I could and discovered a fellow community of like-minded money bloggers. Everyone is a bit different in their blogging niches, so we collaborate and work together. There are money making experts, frugal cooks, deal hunters and coupon experts. So many different bloggers, all focussed on the world of sharing their financial knowledge and creating value for everyone. I immediately felt at home and skipped along to the first event, an Easter Egg tasting event with Quidco.

+

My first paid work

My first paid job as Mrs Mummypenny was in November 2015. I did a lot of work for a small amount of money! I reviewed an app on video, wrote a review post on my site with follow links and ran a competition post for them. All for £50! Seriously though it was such a great project for me to cut my teeth on. I learnt so much from the brand about social media tactics, how to run a competition and how to write a decent review post. They supplied a great competition prize of £100 gift vouchers, so I got great traffic to the post and lots of social likes.

I was always on the search for freebies and deals to post on my Facebook page and website. Soon I had a list of 20-30 ideas for blog posts. I gained more and more confidence that Mrs Mummypenny was a viable business idea that given focus could make a serious amount of cash. I realised it could not just replace my corporate income but make me lots more money than I ever could have earned in employment.

During my deal searching I came across the Aldi Wine Club and joined up in the hope of getting free wine. I was accepted and started to receive free wine in exchange for a tweet review. A few months into the club I received an email asking me to record a 60 second video about my favourite wine to maybe win a chance to film an Aldi wine tasting video.

I went for it and reviewed my favourite sparking sauvignon blanc. My video won and off I went to film wine tasting with Aldi. I met the Clarion PR team and told them all about my website and the Aldi ongoing relationship was born. Every few weeks I review products for them and attend occasional events such as wine tasting pop up shops or new product previews.

I started off working with smaller brands earning £100 per sponsored post. As time went on, I was working with a growing number of brands. I appeared on Bob FM radio as a personal finance expert and I was featured on UK Money Bloggers website. I met more and more PR agencies and brands and my name got around.

After six months

After six months in business I was now working with bigger brands like Standard Life, Compare the Market, Disney, Epson and Smart Energy GB. These jobs came to mostly direct from PR agencies but also direct from brands. I had done all the right things to get my name out there, from attending events to collaborating with other bloggers. Big brands have deeper pockets who will pay more for sponsored posts.

+

After twelve months

I have just passed twelve months trading and am now getting bigger sponsored posts more regularly. I also have a regular stream of affiliate referral income from companies like TopCashback, Amazon and the comparison website uSwitch.

The variety of jobs is exciting and differs from one day to the next. I might review a personal finance app for a start-up company then blog about it one day, or I might review Finding Dory for Disney with a link up to Epson eco-printers. The best bit about blogging is the variety of projects I can be working on at any point in time.

I send out pitches, as it is all part of the process to get your name out there. I have had so many meetings with PR agencies, brands and journalists that have turned into nothing. Sometimes I have spent two hours on a pitch where information has been asked all for me to lose the job to another blogger. Normally one who undercuts me!

I would say maybe one in ten of my outbound pitches or approaches from brands turns into an actual paid piece of work. Some may end up with a lot of time invested for no return. And then other jobs appear in my inbox with a great fee suggested. It's strange how this blogging game works and the fees you can end up getting paid for jobs.

\+

Chapter 5 - What Equipment is Needed to Start Blogging?

The beauty of blogging is that it is open to everyone. The start-up costs are low which makes it perfect for entrepreneurs like you and us. Many blogs, Emma's included, are started on a whim.

In Emma's case a seed was planted, germinated and grew beyond her wildest dreams, which shows that pretty much anyone can turn a dream into reality. To start blogging you will need some practical equipment in addition to oodles of energy, ideas and patience. In this book, we demonstrate how to get started. From that small beginning who knows where you will end up. Blogging has changed our lives for the better in so many ways and it can change yours too.

But becoming a successful blogger and making a good living from the proceeds is not a quick fix. It takes time and a plan but it can be done.

To start your blogging journey, you only need a few things:

- A device for blogging on. This can be a laptop, desktop computer or even a tablet. We both find a laptop is best but there are many blogs that start from a tablet. The only difficulty is that the design setup is trickier on a tablet. However, once set up we know bloggers who even blog on the move via their smartphone!

- A smart phone is an essential tool and ours are pretty much constantly attached to our hands. Smartphones ensure that we can check, update and reply to our followers on social media easily, take photos if required and access emails when on the move. And maybe even answer the odd phone call!

- Going self-hosted is advisable rather than sticking with a free blogging platform like Blogger, as you have more control over your blog. To do this you will need to pay for hosting and design your own blog. There are plenty of templates available to do this so please don't let this put you off starting. Just fill in the blanks and teach yourself the basics as you go along.

- A camera. Many bloggers use their smartphone and this can be perfectly acceptable to start with. Lynn still uses her smartphone and Emma has only just invested in a Canon G7X camera after seven years of blogging. If you want to use lots of images on your blog a camera is a great investment. Emma also uses a Go Pro for filming along with the G7X, but these are not essential when starting out.

- Social media skills. This means setting up Twitter, Instagram, Pinterest, Facebook and any other social media channels you wish to use.

+

- A PayPal account. Many agencies prefer PayPal for payment as it is convenient and quick to administer.

That is it, not too much is it? Blogging really is accessible to almost everyone and it proves that you can start blogging with very little initial outlay. This makes blogging a great business for those with self-belief and entrepreneurial skills. Many people can use their laptops to make money, and reap the benefits for the family life of being self-employed.

+

Chapter 6 - How a Blog Should Look and How Social Media Should Support It

If you are planning to make money from your blog, how it looks is important.

Your blog's appearance creates a first impression before anyone even reads a word of your carefully crafted posts. Your blog needs to look the part, appearing professional and easy to navigate. You don't need to be a great coder or an expert in HTML to make a blog look amazing. There is plenty you can pick up and there are lots of tutorials that will help you develop your skills. Alternatively, if this is an area that you don't enjoy, then pay someone else to do it! Emma has paid others to do the design side of her blog and Lynn has chosen to design hers herself. The blog Emma and 3 has had several headers over the years (a header is the name of your blog at the top of the page) and Emma sees this as investing in her blog.

Many prefer a clean look for a blog, not too cluttered and with a font that is easy to read. Look at your blog from the reader's point of view. Does it look appealing? Would you read your blog? It is also worth asking someone you trust to critique your blog. Can they see anything missing? Do the colours work for them as a reader? Can they navigate it easily?

If you choose to pay someone to build your blog, have clear expectations of what you will receive. We have seen bloggers use freelancers through Fiverr or Etsy and then complain about the quality of the finished banner. If you are paying five pounds for someone to create a banner for you they are likely to be using stock photos and fonts. They will not be spending hours on customising your banner. It is a case of paying for what you get. That said, Emma has used Fiverr for YouTube headers and been pleased with the result.

When recommending a complete blog design, we suggest paying more and getting a personal recommendation. When possible we both use other bloggers or friends who have the skills. It feels good to pass work on to people in a similar position. As a new blogger, you may not know anyone to help and in that situation, we suggest looking at blogs you like and creating a clear brief to give to someone.

It is worth noting that a blog is never finished and therefore do not feel it has to be perfect before you start writing blog posts. Get the basic layout up and ready and then start adding your content. You can play about with design as you get used to your chosen platform. Bloggers are always tinkering away behind the scenes!

+

There are a few technical blogging terms that we have used in this chapter and they are defined in the glossary at the end of the book.

Getting started and choosing a platform

There are several platforms available with Blogger and WordPress being the most popular. Blogger is owned by Google and complements other Google products. However, you never own the site and technically it could be taken down by Google at any time. The big advantage though is that Blogger is free and easy to navigate. Many PR and SEO agencies will not work with blogs with a BlogSpot/WordPress in their web address (URL).

This can be overcome by purchasing a vanity URL which takes the BlogSpot out of the address. Having a BlogSpot address also means that you cannot get Domain Authority (DA) and DA is how some agencies choose which bloggers to work with on a campaign. WordPress also have a free option but a bloggers are not allowed to take paid collaborations on wordpress.org. For these reasons, we suggest going self-hosted from the start or moving to this option as soon as possible.

+

Being self-hosted means that you have to pay for your hosting and that you are responsible for setting it up, updating files and doing back-ups. However, don't think it needs to be expensive. Hosting can cost under £10 a month and buying a domain name costs about the same per year. There are too many hosting companies to name but TSO, LCN and EvoHosting are popular with bloggers that we know.

Choosing a name

This is where Emma will hold her hand up and say that she chose a name without any consideration. Emma and 3 was born in an instant without pre-planning and coming up with a clever name. She kind of wishes it had a different name, but now it has become her brand and is too well known for a change. The 3 represents the three children but that is about as clever as it gets.

Lynn had a different approach to choosing the name and it was the one of her first decisions when creating the blog. She sat down with a friend with a brilliant marketing and creative mind and a bottle of wine. Then they brainstormed. They came up with idea after idea and until they found a name that they both loved. Mrs Mummypenny was born.

Lynn loves the name, but it's not without its issues. People often look for Mrs Moneypenny (a completely different person!) and there are a few parenting bloggers with similar names. The very next day after choosing the names the blog went live, hosting was set up and social media channels were obtained.

Before you press "buy" on your domain name we suggest checking all the social media channels to see if they are available and only then should you go ahead with your purchase. Ideally you want to set up Twitter, Instagram, Pinterest and Facebook account all using the same name. Having the social channels makes your brand consistent and easily recognisable.

Once you have bought your URL consider buying the other domain endings. Next redirect them or point at your site. You really do not want someone else buying the co.uk when you are using the .com version and you also don't want to have a very similar name to someone else. We advise Googling any names you consider and seeing what the searches bring up before purchasing anything.

+

Choosing a colour scheme

The colours you use on your blog can have an impact on how it is viewed. There have been many pieces of research that look at colours and how it affects our mood. Using colours that work together is important. You are encouraging your readers to have a pleasant experience after all.

Red: energy, passion, excitement, power; also implies aggression, danger.

Blue: coolness, spirituality, freedom, patience, loyalty, peace, trustworthiness; can also sadness, depression.

Yellow: light, optimism, happiness, brightness, joy.

Green: life, naturalness, restfulness, health, wealth, prosperity; in certain contexts, can imply decay, toxicity.

Orange: friendliness, warmth, approachability, energy, playfulness, courage.

Violet: wisdom, sophistication, celebration.

White: purity, cleanliness, youth, freshness, peace.

Black: power, elegance, secrecy, mystery.

Grey: security, maturity, reliability.

Pink: romance, a feminine colour.

Brown: comfort, strength, stability, credibility.

Once you have decided on the colour palette you can use services to help find the exact shade and which colours it naturally partners with. Don't ignore these features as they can affect the success of your site on a psychological level.

When you expand and have more than one blog it is a good idea to have some colour consistency across them. This is something that Emma only recently thought about and she has now linked Emma and 3, Mums Savvy Savings and her YouTube header using similar colours. Emma and 3 for a long time used pastel colours but as she is writing more about education, empowering girls and health she has moved to bolder, stronger colours which suit her topics. Both blogs now use blue and teal colours demonstrating trustworthiness and loyalty which are important characteristics to Emma.

Emma and 3 has moved away from a parenting focus as the children have got older and she writes less about being a mum. Emma therefore made a considered decision to switch colours as the blog moved from parenting to more of a lifestyle blog. Using the same colours and same photo across the blogs creates uniformity, and enables readers to see the blogs are linked.

Mrs Mummypenny uses a colour palette of purple and green. Lynn's favourite colour is purple which was the main motivation of colour choice. It's often associated with royalty, nobility, luxury, power and ambition. Purple also represents meanings of wealth, extravagance and creativity which is perfect for a personal finance and lifestyle blog. The green went perfectly with the purple and is meant to represent health, wealth and prosperity.

What pages do you need on the blog?

Once you have decided to go for a self-hosted blog, you need to choose a theme. A theme is the blog design, and depends on your personal choice. Many bloggers use magazine templates for their theme, as it is a modern design.

Some bloggers update their theme on a regular basis, at least once a year but some will keep the same theme for years. There are plenty of free themes available and we suggest you start with those (we are money bloggers after all). You can also pay for a more customisable theme but the choice is yours. Look at blogs and decide from there what type of theme you like. Things to include:

- **Homepage.** The homepage is where the most recent posts are seen. Depending on your theme you can have the whole post showing or just an excerpt.

- **Categories**. Blog posts should be categorised and grouped together depending on their topic. The categories are then listed under or above your header. This makes it easier for readers to navigate and find similar posts. Categories could include parenting, travel or food, it depends on what you blog about.

- **About Me**. This gives readers and brands personal information about you. It could detail your children's ages (if applicable), where you live (town but not address) and how to contact you. This page lets others know your interests and how you might fit in with their campaigns so make sure that it is positive and showcases you well.

+

- **Work with Me**. This page should explain ways in which you will work with brands and could showcase some of your previous collaborations. You could include any testimonials from people that you have worked with previously. You may wish to advertise the type of collaborations you are interested in. Emma for example lists public speaking as she enjoys it and sees it as a strength of hers. This page is your selling place, where you inform others what you can do for them. It is not a place to be shy so tell the world how fabulous you are.

- **Disclosure**. Set out your terms and conditions clearly on a page, especially if you run competitions on your blog. This is where you show that you are complying with advertising rules. You can also use this page to explain whether you use affiliate links in posts.

In the Sidebar

- **Photo and brief bio**. The sidebar also needs to be well used as it appears on every page in the blog. Many bloggers include a photograph of themselves with a brief biography. Using the same photograph across your blog and social media channels helps you become instantly recognisable. Using a photo also helps readers identify with you, and it shows that you are a real person with a personality rather than a faceless unknown. We suggest you invest in a professional profile headshot rather than a selfie.

- **Links to your social media channels**. It is important to make it easy for readers to follow you on all your social media channels. Growing your social media channels can be as important as the words you write. Your audience is often measured in terms of how many followers you have. Search for widgets to include on your blog that do the linking for you. Just add your user names and then they link up.

- **A Search bar**. From a PR angle a search bar allows brands to see if you have written about their product. It also allows people to find posts on your blog quickly.

- **A Subscribe button**. Many bloggers encourage readers to subscribe and they then receive new posts directly to their inbox as an email. This can ensure regular readers do not miss a post.

- **Badges** Include badges to show which blogger networks you belong to. The badges are often important for the networks themselves. So for example the Tot's100 badge tracks visitor numbers which is how their charts are calculated. Mumsnet insists on bloggers having the badge if they work on paid campaigns as it advertises the Mumsnet blogger network.

+

- **Adverts**. Many bloggers include adverts in the sidebar of their blogs, whether from Google Adsense or by working directly with companies. Google Adsense pay depending on how many people see the advert. This can provide a passive income but obviously the amount depends on traffic and page views.

- **Social media feeds**. Some bloggers include feeds showing recent tweets, recent Instagram photos and recent posts. It's down to personal choice. Think about what you like to see in other websites or what frustrates you when it's not there. Lynn's biggest frustration is when the search bar is hard to find or doesn't exist. Also, when a website is too cluttered with too many things in the side panel or too content heavy in the main navigation bar.

Under Posts

Don't forget to add a widget under each post showing similar posts. If you read one of Emma's hip dysplasia posts, underneath the post you would see clickable links to other similar posts on hip dysplasia that she has written previously. Encouraging readers to read another post on the blog will reduce your bounce rate and increase your page views.

You can also use other widgets to add share buttons underneath your posts. These allow readers to share your post directly to other social media channels. For many this is a huge traffic boost and ensures your post is shared widely, again this will increase your reach and page views.

Images

Images break up text and as the old cliché goes a picture is worth a thousand words. Images help tell a story so do include images in your posts. As for size the bigger the better, we both try to keep all our images the same size to create a uniform look across our blogs. We personally aim for 600 by 600 pixels as the optimum size.

Many themes grab an image to use as insert on the home page. This is called a feature image and accompanies the introduction to the text. This is the image social media often grabs too. Make sure the picture is relevant and adds to the story. When writing a sponsored post for a brand, and they will often provide an image upon request.

If you don't have a suitable picture you might choose to use one from another blogger. Always ask permission and remember, it is good etiquette to link back and credit the blogger.

+

Another alternative is to use a stock photo and there are many sites offering free image including Unsplash and Pixabay. You can also use images from Google provided you select the image option – images- usage rights - labelled for reuse.

Many bloggers use Canva as a source of images. Canva allows you to edit images and you can add wording and watermarks with your blog name. You can also create different image sizes, which is particularly useful for Pinterest where image size is important.

Which Social Media Channels To Use?

We suggest using the ones that you like. The primary benefits of social media channels are to help promote your blog posts and to engage with your readers and followers. It is a way to share your content and talk to those that read your posts. Recently, it is also becoming more commonplace to be paid to post directly onto social media channels.

Digital influencers are growing alongside bloggers, and people are now being paid directly to host content on their social media channels. On Instagram for example some influencers, with substantial followers, are being paid hundreds of pounds to include a picture on their Instagram feed.

Takumi pay digital influencers on a sliding scale that is directly proportional to how many followers you have. You can also get paid for tweets on Twitter and vlogs on YouTube, just ensure you are complying with ASA Guidelines and declaring these relationships with #AD or #Sponsored as directed by the network. Look out for paid opportunities that require posting on your social media channels.

Please be warned that buying followers is never recommended and people who pay just to inflate their social following numbers just look daft. It is obvious when followers have been bought as engagement is low and a brief look at the followers show that they are not real people. Instagram regularly clears out these accounts too which just makes you look like a fraud! Building social media channels takes time and is always work in progress. There are no shortcuts to putting in the time and effort.

Social media channels that bloggers frequently use include:

- Twitter is a great platform to have a conversation on. Do remember to talk to others and not just post your links without any personal comments. If you use it just to share links you will not see much growth or engagement. Alice Talbot Judge from More Than Toast gives this tip top:

+

Twitter is an incredible tool, not just for regurgitating links to your websites, but for forging a meaningful two-way relationship with your audience and customers. It's easy to forget that it's not just a broadcasting platform and is instead one to maximise engagement and loyalty... think of your account as a stage, somewhere to put forward your best self in front of a rapt audience, eager to respond.

- Facebook. Having a fan page can encourage your posts to be shared. It is often due to Facebook that posts go viral as they are shared and debated across the platform. Growing Facebook can be hard work but Emma Mumford the Coupon Queen and This Morning contributor gives the following tip:

Growing your Facebook page takes time and dedication. I have over 240k followers since starting back in September 2013. The main ways I have grown my Facebook page are through finding what works, it's all about creating engaging content as this is what attracts new followers and readers to your blog. Competitions also work really well and are a great way to reward your readers, also posting meme's and articles of interest which get people talking is another great way to grow your following.

- YouTube is a video and visual platform, with the potential for high earnings. Brands often pay two or three times more for a vlog than they do for a sponsored post. A vlogger is Emma Conway from Brummy Mummy of Two. Emma suggests having a regular time and day for uploading new content. Also, plan your vlogs like you would a post. Remember that your channel should have a header, use keywords and rich descriptions. Emma gives this great advice:

Consistency and titling your video correctly. Think of your favourite TV show? You know that it is on twice a week at a certain time. Apply this to your channel. Your subscribers will be waiting for a video and if you post it at a random time it make get lost. Also be authentic and original. YouTube can provide ANYONE with an audience. That's its beauty!

- Instagram is another visual platform that can help readers see more of you. Using hashtags alongside the images will help people find your content and engage with you. Harriet from Toby and Roo gives this advice and considering she had over 30K followers at last look she knows her Instagram stuff!

My tip is about posting and trying to maximise the time after by focusing on the correct hashtags. So for example; I use #littlefierceones and then go into that tag, comment and like the top 9, followed by perhaps 10-20 of the most recently posted.

+

Doing that really engages with the people that you want to come and see your photo and it is a fab way to help boost your own numbers as chances are the people who have just posted to that tag are still in app and if you engage with them they are more likely to return the favour.

- Pinterest is a huge traffic source for many bloggers. For Pinterest to be beneficial you do need to invest time into creating pinnable images an optimum size is 735 by 1335 pixels. These images should be vertical and again a description is important for a pin to show up in searches.

Becky Goddard Hill from Family Budgeting has amassed over 200K followers on Pinterest and her advice is:

Pinterest takes time and dedication and like all social media a minimum daily 15 minutes works well. Using a scheduler like Tailwind is a huge time saver. Read blog posts on pinning tips so you are sending the right sized images and maximising your exposure. Essentially Pinterest is a search tool so your descriptions and titles need to be full of keywords that people that people would search for and your images need to be good quality and vertical.

- LinkedIn is a professional network primarily used by businesses. LinkedIn is a good place to share blog

+

posts that are on a specific topic for example education or small business tips. LinkedIn is not the place for potty reviews though.

- Snapchat is considered by many to be a tool of the youth! It allows a more personal look into the lives of bloggers and many brands use Snapchat to connect with people.

- Google+ was once expected to become the biggest social media channel but never really got there. As it is a Google product using Google+ has an impressive impact on SEO. Using Google+ to promote posts will help a post come up higher in the search results so it is worth having a profile and using it.

Once your social channels are up and running it is time to use them. Use your channels to engage with and to grow your audience. Do not just dump links and run as this will not help organic growth. Take time to talk and share other people's content, not just your own. There are tools like Tweet Deck and Buffer that allow you to schedule updates to Twitter and Facebook. These can be useful for pushing out posts and sharing them. You upload your post and set the time for the tweet or status to be published. This can also be useful for pushing out your evergreen posts on topics that never date. Add time into your day to schedule these posts but be careful not to overload your timelines and appear spammy. We suggest on the day a post is published share it to Twitter three or four times that day. Research suggests the impact of a tweet only lasts eight minutes.

How your blog looks and is presented can make or break success. Our suggestions will get you off to a flying start. You may have been blogging for a while and are looking to step it up, if this is the case implement what we have said and with some hard work you will see positive outcomes.

We are all still able to improve and grow our blogs no matter how long we have been doing it. Emma and Lynn both continue to invest time, energy and money into their blogs as this ensures future success.

Use this page to make notes on what you need to implement.   Now number them in order of priority.

Chapter 7 - Networking for Ultimate Success

The phrase 'It's not what you know it's who you know' is used often in the world of networking. The world of marketing and PR is a relatively small world and once you become known by a few big agencies and other bloggers you can progress.

It pays huge dividends in any environment to be professional, friendly and helpful. Emma and Lynn are both known within their circles of ex-professional worlds and the blogger world to possess these characteristics. Help that we have given to others will mostly be repaid (although not always!). Favours that you do for others will come back two-fold. Work life then becomes so much easier when you have people to support you in new projects.

There are so many times in the past year for Lynn and several years for Emma where networking has helped hugely with each person's blogging world. From our groups where we are active members or to groups that we have set up, to blogging networking events and to brand events. Our approach to each event is always with the same attitude, professionalism, friendliness and interest in others.

The lonely world of blogging? We don't think so

Blogging is often perceived to be a lonely world. We work mostly from home, in the box bedroom or corner of the dining room. We spend our lives typing away on the laptop or have our heads buried in our phone or tablet. Blogging life can be like this if you want it. The blogging life we have chosen to embrace is the group life of bloggers. We have both built networks with other bloggers in a similar field to us. We both collaborate with similar niche bloggers sharing content between sites.

An example of networking and taking opportunities offered can be easily demonstrated by Emma. Two years ago, Emma was invited by the Mark Warner PR team to go for breakfast and cocktails before Britmums Live. Emma had already sorted her travel but decided it was worth the £50 to change her ticket. She attended breakfast with a few other bloggers on a Friday morning, the following Wednesday Emma and her family were invited on a press trip to spend a week in Corsica courtesy of Mark Warner. By Sunday morning Emma and the children were on a British Airways flight to spend a glorious week sailing and reviewing a Mark Warner holiday. All because Emma accepted that networking opportunity!

Facebook Groups

Join in with the blogging Facebook groups. If you can't find one for your niche engage with other bloggers on Twitter and ask which groups they are part of. The best group for the personal finance niche is UK Money Bloggers. It is a small but perfectly formed group where we ask questions, share information and celebrate each other's success. As mentioned in previous chapters much of the technical things we have learned have come from that Facebook group.

All sorts of exciting stuff has come from the UK Money Bloggers group that we are both part of. A highlight was the UK Money blogger SHOMO awards held in September 2016. The day was packed with amazing content from blogging experts and brands and a room full of 50 bloggers who rarely get an opportunity to meet up together.

Being with likeminded bloggers and small business people can be incredibly inspiring, after all one of the ideas that came out of the event was this book! Speak to as many people as possible and ask questions and then more questions.

Find out how people are doing business wise and how they have got to their blogging position if they are doing well. Touch base with people who you engaged with and got on well with afterwards. Drop them a tweet and/or share a few of their posts. Maybe write a blog post about the event and name drop a few people.

The network you build here will help you vastly in the short term for blog improvement ideas and in the longer term. As you stay connected to these people they may recommend you for jobs to brands where they have a relationship. We will both often work with brands who ask for blogger recommendations, of course we will recommend those whom we have collaborated with on blog posts in the past. We will recommend those who we have trusted relationship with and there is no substitute for meeting people in the flesh and having a great chat to them.

Blogging Events

There are several big events and award shows that are a great idea to attend, particularly in the early days of blogging. These can feel scary and we might be put off going. The events are typically incredibly well run with very little time standing around where you might be scared of having no one to talk to.

+

A great event in November every year is the Mumsnet Blogfest event and awards. It was the first big event that Lynn attended early on in her blogging career. She felt a bit like a fraud going, worried that she would know no one with her tiny blog with no earnings and small social media numbers. There was no need to worry as Blogfest was a very well run event with lots of great seminars and theatre talks. There were lots of brands there to chat to with freebies galore, and there were 300 bloggers attending. Lynn sought out every blogger that she admired and respected and approached them and told them so. There were a few fan moments with bloggers that she now considers friends.

Another great event is the Tots 100 MAD blog awards. Emma as the editor of Tots 100 was very much a part of this day and was up for an exciting award. The awards have many categories and being a finalist is a great accolade and looks impressive on your blogging CV. It demonstrates that you are at the top of the game. The MAD blog awards is a red-carpet event held in a beautiful five-star hotel in central London and celebrates everything good and wonderful about blogging – why not set yourself a goal of getting an invite?

Brand Events

As your blog progresses, you will start to get invited to all sorts of exciting events and we recommend that you go to as many as you can. When you are there work hard to build a relationship with the brands and the PR agencies. These are the guys that have found your blogs, worked out you are the perfect fit and invited you to the event. Well maintained relationships will mean that these guys will commission more work from you, invite you to more events and include you in more blogger outreach campaigns.

There are many cooler than cool events from the past year in Lynn's blogging life but one highlight was an Aldi event where much wine was tasted and discussed in an Aldi Wine pop-up shop in Shoreditch. By this point there was already a solid relationship with the PR agency nurtured through collaborative projects and promotions for Aldi. The event was a press event so there were a wide variety of writers, journalists, event organisers and TV people around. Lynn worked the room and made some fantastic connections which have subsequently turned into paid work. Again, it's not what you know it's who you know.

Emma has been to some amazing events over the years and met many celebrities. Highlights have been spa days with Next, lunch at the top of the BT tower and VIP experiences at festivals. However, ask the children what their favourite from the past year has been and Dylan would say being invited to the FA Cup Semi Finals. The girls would say being guests of Vodafone at the Summertime Capital Ball. Along with Sally the founder of Tots100.

Small Business & Entrepreneur Networks

It's important to keep things local and build relationships with local business people in different industries. You never know what you can learn from the local butcher, sign maker or florist. If it's a business that is established and has been on your local high street for a while they are probably doing OK. You might even get some work from these companies if they need some social media or marketing help. You are after all building a brand in the digital world and could be the perfect place to promote their business.

The Federation of Small Business offer lots of networking opportunities if you join up. Lean In, the Sheryl Sandberg movement, also runs groups all over the country and events are free to attend.

+

Corporate Network

Lynn can reflect on the past year in blogging business and see that a vast amount of the success and jobs that she has worked on has been from her networking. Part of that networking success is a due to the corporate network she has built up from HSBC, Tesco and EE. LinkedIn has been a brilliant tool for maintaining those corporate relationships and how to keep in touch with ex colleagues. She has been known to send a message to a colleague from eight years ago who now works at John Lewis to try to work out how to get into that company to pitch. It never does any harm to ask.

Chapter 8 – How to Set Goals to Drive Success

When your blog is your business it is important to have structure and a strategy. It's your own business so you need to treat it seriously and plan for every eventuality. Goal setting can be a really positive and direction based way of planning.

By this point you have your basics settled and agreed. You know why you want to blog and you have a passion for creating a business for that blog. Now is a great time to dream big and set those big aspirational goals of where you could get with your blog.

There is a school of thought that if you dream big you will get there. Aspire to huge things that you might not think are possible. Aim to earn £100,000 and if you get to £50,000 you have done an incredible thing.

Overarching ambition

Think about what you really want from your business. How can you describe your ambition in one sentence? Maybe it is about creating work/life balance. Maybe it's about creating an income from a flexible job. Maybe it's about becoming an expert in a field and helping others. Have a think about your one big super goal, what you are passionate about and/or what drives you to write every day.

For Lynn, it's to become a leading personal finance expert in the country. For Emma, it's being recognised as an authority on blogging.

Big Goals

Big goals for your business will relate to a period of time, maybe the next year, six months, or maybe three months. It's often best to plan forward as far as you can. After all, you would take a mortgage deal for five years so why not think about the five-year plan for your business. Now there is a challenge!

We would recommend coming up with two-three big goals. Maybe one relating to your blog/brand and one relating to your earnings. Remember, these need to be a challenge, and something way bigger than you think possible. It could be one of these

- To earn £1,000 in the first six months of running your blog
- To have your blog/brand earn enough money to replace your current employed earnings
- To quit your employed job and to become a full-time blogger
- To grow your brand to have social reach of 10,000
- To have 20,000 unique views of your website per month
- To be earning £5,000 per month from your blog/brand

- To be considered the expert in your blogging/writing field
- To work with particular brands you admire and respect
- To appear on BBC Breakfast or This Morning as an expert in your field

Lynn's two big goals are:

1) Generate turnover of £5,000 per month
2) Grow brand presence.

Emma's three big goals are:

1) Generate turnover of £5,000 per month consistently
2) Speak as an authority on blogging
3) Join big campaigns including more media opportunities.

Shorter term goals

Next take each big goal and break it down into parts. Be brave and write down all the possibilities. Once you have those options go through, prioritise and focus on those that make you happy and you know you will enjoy doing.

The great thing about these shorter-term goals is that you can make them SMART, and you will know when you have achieved them.

Smart stands for:

- Specific
- Measurable
- Achievable
- Relevant
- Timely

For example:

If your goal is to grow your blog and brand presence, your quarterly objectives could be:

1) Focus on building your Facebook page and groups up to 5,000 members and likes
2) Build your Twitter followers to 10,000
3) Build your Instagram followers to 5,000
4) Set up a YouTube channel and build subscribers to 1,000
5) Create an email database with 5,000 subscribers
6) Appear in print media
7) Build collaborative relationships with five other bloggers in your niche

You would then go through and prioritise these. To prioritise, use a points scheme of importance and urgency ratings. This will then give you a great idea on what to focus on every day.

+

Daily goals

Let's focus on one of the short-term quarterly goals and break it down into daily tasks - Build your Facebook page and group membership to 5,000 members.

This was one of Lynn's first goals relating to her brand. She knew that Facebook was important to the growth of her brand and was the most popular social media choice for her demographic. She worked hard to grow her Facebook profile and likes.

For Lynn, it included things like:

1) Share all blog posts on your Facebook page and encourage sharing
2) Run a competition where 'sharing is caring'
3) Pay for Facebook advertising to put your brand in front of people interested in your niche
4) Collaborate with other bloggers who will share your work
5) Ask brands to share your Facebook page on their Facebook page
6) Comment on relevant Facebook groups and share your page details
7) Set up Facebook member groups – e.g. Mrs Mummypenny Money Saving Tips
8) Set up a Facebook post schedule and vary your posts every day

+

9) Get engaging conversations going on your page with lots of people commenting
10) Analyse your Facebook insights to understand your most popular posts

All the above can be incorporated into your daily to-do list and all relate back to your short-term goals, long term goals and overarching master goal.

Every day we like to write a to-do list. It works best to only list three or four things. As we go through the day we know we will get distracted and end up doing other things, so these make it onto the to-do list when they have been done. That way we can see what has been achieved, the initial three to four things plus a load more other stuff.

Both Emma and Lynn find that they are always extremely effective and motivated earlier in the week so load more working hours and important tasks into the beginning of the week. Thursdays and Fridays are great days for face to face meetings and catching up.

+

What are your goals?

List three short term goals

1

2

3

List two long term goals

1

2

Chapter 9 - How to Work with PR and SEO Agencies

The goal of many bloggers is to monetise their blogs and earn a good living from the opportunities it can bring. Both Emma and Lynn have achieved this, with both leaving previous careers to achieve what they see as the perfect work life balance. The aim for both was to be able to work for themselves, not to feel the guilt, not to miss school assemblies and sports days and yet still bring in an income that at least matches what they were earning in previous employment.

To achieve this, they quickly recognised that building solid relationships with PR agencies and SEO agencies was key, as they are the gatekeepers to the mystical brand opportunities. We were both determined to work with agencies that will keep coming back time and time again because they know we deliver promises on time and to a high standard.

Firstly, it is essential to know the difference between PR and SEO. PR agencies work with bloggers to promote products and services, SEO or Search Engine Optimisation agencies are different in that their role is to generate online links and build up the search terms of a product or service. Both work with bloggers across all niches and these relationships are one of the most popular ways to earn money from blogging.

+

PR agencies may contact bloggers directly and offer them goods to review. Think toys in readiness for Christmas or clothes in preparation for season change overs and you will be on the right lines. These reviews can be mutually beneficial, as bloggers are usually given the item to keep in exchange for their time creating a blog post and sharing the post to their online audience. Bloggers may also be paid for this service by PR agencies and it is always worth asking if there is a budget in addition to the product. If you don't ask you don't get! Reviewing products is often the first interaction a blogger has with agencies.

SEO is different because this is more often paid for campaigns where you link to the brand or product. You are less likely to receive the product but will be paid for the campaign. Google do have guidelines on this which are discussed in chapter 14. Ensure you know the guidelines and decide which is right for you and your brand.

As a new blogger, it is often a goal to get onto the PR agency list. Most agencies genuinely have an actual list to share contact details of bloggers with high engagement or a niche area.

PR Execs also move agencies frequently and they will take their contacts with them therefore it is really important that you always remain professional as your details will travel around agencies. It is also not uncommon to work with several people from one agency as Execs are often responsible for specific clients and they will recommend you for briefs if you do your job well.

How to get on a PR's radar

There are many ways to get your blog and your name noticed and this next section shares what has worked for us. Follow these tips and you too will be approached by PR's.

Write good content

It seems obvious but it is the first and most important part of being noticed by agencies. Agencies read blogs, and spend their time selecting the best bloggers for their clients and campaigns. Their reputation depends on picking the right blogs for the campaign and so they do their research.

A PR contact has shared one of her secrets. Friday afternoon is her blog reading time. It is during this time she comes across new bloggers to work with and this is when she makes notes of bloggers details. This goes to show that agencies are always on the lookout for new talent – don't assume they use the same people time and time again.

Bloggers who regularly write good content will always be ahead of the game as they will shine and stand out to agencies. The reason agencies want to work with bloggers is because bloggers have influence and this influence can lead to sales and increased brand trust. Newer bloggers can feel that they need to make their mark and start earning from collaborations within weeks of setting up a blog. This very rarely happens and you need to prove your worth – remember you will be receiving products that cost money to the brand so keep writing regularly and the opportunities will follow.

Writing about a niche topic

Writing on a niche topic will help brands recognise who your audience is.

Many parent bloggers worry about not having a niche but they often do, it is just that they haven't identified it themselves. The niche could be as broad as parenting but that is still a niche, it is talking to other parents about parenting?

When a parenting brand is looking to promote a product, they will seek parenting blogs. Your niche might be very specific and that is fine too. You may worry that having a niche narrows down potential collaborations but in our experience, that is not the case.

Personal finance for example is niche but there are many companies wanting to work with bloggers that can give money advice from budgeting to frugal recipes. Having a niche can help you make an impact. Emma and Lynn are the go to bloggers for personal finance and money saving campaigns for many brands. Agencies are aware of our niche areas of content. From Emma's personal point of view it is why she has two blogs, she wanted to separate the niches early on. Emma and 3 has an education, parenting and health background and Mums Savvy Savings is about all things relating to money.

Comment on other blogs

In the past we have been offered collaborations directly because of commenting on other blogs. Good PR agencies will monitor and follow conversations on social media channels. If you want to work with a brand that you can see other bloggers are working on, comment and share those posts. You will often be seen by the PR and this could lead to future collaborations. A word of warning do not write spam comments or ask to work with the brand on someone else's post as it can look desperate. Bloggers also don't appreciate other bloggers dropping links within their comments unless they are through comment systems like comment Luv. Instead, make thoughtful comments which will be appreciated by both the blogger and the brand.

Reviewing Products

If you would like to carry out reviews on your blog start by reviewing things that you already own or are doing. That could be a toy review or reviewing places you visit as a family. This will give you experience in writing up reviews and how to structure them. This will also demonstrate to PR Execs that you are open to reviewing on your blog. It is another way to get noticed for the things that you want to do.

Press Releases

Press releases are often sent to bloggers as your details are added to all types of lists. Many of these press releases are sent out generically and it would be difficult to reply to everyone. When we are approached directly with a personalised email we always reply. Set up a stock reply and send it back to approaches. If the topic is not relevant just say that, thank them for the information and move on. However, many press releases can be relevant and by replying you will be connecting with the brand. It can lead to work opportunities especially if you suggest how you can work together. Ask if there is a budget for the campaign, ask if samples are available for review purposes and you might have just landed another campaign. You will need to be proactive as a successful blogger and grab opportunities as they land in your inbox.

Email Approach

Email brands and agencies that you would like to collaborate with and introduce yourself. Don't jump straight in with a pitch, but simply introduce yourself in a brief email and add your media kit. A media kit should have your relevant statistics and a little about you. Ask to be added to any databases of bloggers for upcoming campaigns.

+

One successful way that we have used to develop new working relationships is by asking a fellow blogger to make an introduction. This can be very influential especially if the brand has an ongoing relationship with the blogger in question. For example, if either of us have been commissioned for a money saving post and if the brand is still looking for other bloggers with similar demographics and in the same topic area we will share the contact details of other trusted bloggers. This demonstrates that we are an expert or authority in our blogging niche and recognise others who are trustworthy and experts. It also often means that they return the favour and introduce you to brands that they may be working with. Blogging is a very social job, the more you integrate and support others, the more it will be returned.

Events

Events are a great way to become known to other bloggers and brands. Networking is a powerful tool when used correctly. It always amazes us when bloggers say they are shy or can't talk to agencies on the phone. If you want to be a successful blogger it is crucial you overcome that hurdle. We suggest reading up on how to look confident. Fake it until you feel it!

Lynn is very happy and confident to speak to agencies on the phone so suggests the following:-

1) Ask if they have spare five minutes to talk

+

2) Introduce your blog and your niche
3) Share how you can help them with their campaign.

Just let the conversation flow. Be natural, enthusiastic and it will get you far.

Blogging is as much about community as it is about writing. Events provide the chance to meet other bloggers in person and develop those relationships. Attend what you can and always introduce yourself to people and give out your business cards.

Events often fall into two camps, the first are press events that are drop in pop up events, Christmas in July is a prime example of these. They are open to all sections of the press and you drop in during the day and see new products about to be launched. Many are held in London and you are not likely to be given travel expenses for these events but goody bags are usually provided.

The second type of event is a bloggers event. These will be by invitation and are with a set objective and timeframe. At blogger events travel expenses are often covered so do ask before committing yourself.

Over the years we have been to some fabulous events including being invited to the top of the BT Tower with Internet Safety which is no longer open to visitors unless by invitation, spa treatments with Next at a lovely venue.

More recently a chocolate making workshop at The Savoy Hotel with Tena. Both Emma and Lynn really enjoyed learning how to make chocolate flowers at that one despite neither of them being very good at it!

Blog Conferences

Blog conferences provide a great opportunity to connect with brands and agencies. There are now many conferences in the blogging calendar, including something for everyone from smaller conferences on a specific niche to all-encompassing huge events where hundreds of bloggers will descend. More and more UK bloggers are also going overseas for conferences especially those held in America where blogging could be argued to be a few years ahead of us in the UK. Many of the conferences are held in London but BlogCamp is held in Birmingham, Blog On in Manchester and more are appearing all the time.

There has also been a rise in niche conferences to meet the needs of bloggers, for example the UK Money Blogger SHOMOs conference is heading into its third year and is a smaller conference for those blogging about money. Blog Stock is aimed at creative types and has an excellent reputation too. There really is a conference for everyone. Brands often pay to attend conferences either to mingle with bloggers and make connections or via a stand where they are looking to work with bloggers.

Ensure that you take business cards to all conferences, we rarely leave the house without some in our wallet. Conferences are often very busy and it can feel like a competition to connect with a brand but hold your head high and engage. We take business cards from the brand too and will then follow up with a polite email a few days later and have built many a relationship from meeting brands at conferences. It is also worth entering the competitions on offer at these events, in the past Emma has won a Vitamix and a holiday from being at Britmums!

+

Facebook

Facebook groups are a great tool for growing your blog and connecting with brands. Arguably Facebook is one of the hardest networks to grow but Facebook groups themselves can really help a blogger. There are many groups and we suggest joining lots and deciding which one works for you. Facebook groups often have opportunities posted in them and it is another way of getting your details passed over to agencies.

Another tip is that if you review or write a post about a brand start a conversation on their Facebook page and leave a link. Remember not to spam so only do this once but hopefully the person running the Facebook page will engage and they may even share the post more widely.

Twitter

Twitter is a great place to talk directly to brands. Follow brands that you would like to work with. Share their tweets and engage with them online. If you write a post that would interest a brand tag them in the tweet as it often opens-up a conversation.

It is worth noting that not all Twitter accounts are handled by the PR agencies, some may subcontract their social media but it is still a valid way of making contact. Your posts being retweeted from a brand can drive traffic to your blog too which is always appreciated.

Secondly use Twitter to search hashtags, opportunities often crop up from searches that include #bloggerswanted or #prrequest. Bloggers have had lots of success and made preliminary introductions over Twitter. Another tip is once you have engaged with a brand via Twitter and want to pitch an idea to them ask for an email address rather than conducting it over a public space.

Finally, be professional. We have shared what we consider being professional means but as we have said PR Execs move about and with it does your reputation. Be known for being pleasant, professional and reliable and you will find PR Exec's suggesting you for campaigns and PR Exec's coming back to work with you time and time again.

Fostering those relationships are crucial as when you are self-employed chasing work takes up valuable time. If clients are coming to you, take the compliment that you are doing a great job.

+

In the past Emma has been given work because she has been seen as having a great online personality. She steers clear of public spats, doesn't swear online and always behaves in a professional manner and this gets noticed. We both want brands talking about us for the right reasons and that means being professional. We also know of brands that will not work with bloggers they have been told don't deliver or court controversy online. Your reputation is one of your most important selling points so look after it!

Chapter 10 - How and When to Pitch to PR Agencies

When you write good regular content and build up your audience, brands will approach you for a huge range of opportunities from sponsored posts to attending events.

However, you do not have to wait to be approached. You can be proactive and contact brands that you want to collaborate with yourself. In the past bloggers have been accused of blagging but now we call that pitching. It has taken a while for bloggers to get the recognition they deserve and to feel confident as an industry in approaching agencies but the tide has turned. Although there are tried and tested ways to go about pitching, it is a skill that can be developed and improved. Just as you would negotiate on a price for a paid campaign, there are ways to go about putting a pitch together and in this section will we share our own tips on what has worked for us.

When to pitch

One of the fundamental pieces of advice is not to expect too much too soon.

Both Emma and Lynn have seen first-hand in Facebook groups where very new bloggers, often with only a few posts, ask for advice about why brands are not contacting them. We suggest implementing our tips from How to work with PR's and SEO agencies first. This chapter, How and When to Pitch is aimed at bloggers with over six-months experience. It is for bloggers who have shown that they are committed to blogging and that they are not just out for a freebie. When very new bloggers jump in with pitches it can be detrimental to the blogging community as a whole. Learn your trade first, apply for opportunities you see but save cold calling until you have more experience.

The time to consider pitching is when you have something to offer as it is a two-way relationship. Lynn started pitching with Mrs Mummypenny after nine months of building the blog. The PR and brand will look carefully at your blog, your social media and what you can offer. Consider what you can offer the brand and why they should work with you. Remember, if they are going to give you something to review or pay for your time from their budget they will want to know why they should spend time and money on you.

+

When you pitch put together a comprehensive proposal to outline why you are the best person to review or write the post. Having a niche and focus helps with this. Many brands and PR's know that if they have Education type clients then it will fit very well on Emma and 3 as Emma is an ex-teacher who writes about education regularly. You will see many posts on reviewing educational resources or providing post school options. The same with Mrs Mummypenny brands recognise that Lynn is an expert, an authority on money matters and any post about personal finance sits effortlessly on her blog. A new niche within a niche appears to be energy budgeting, switching and branded campaigns. When you see these trends and authority building like this work it into pitches.

Lynsey Devon, Founder and Chief Executive of Heaven Publicity explains what she looks for when recruiting bloggers for campaigns.

When approaching bloggers for campaigns I look for high engagement with readers this will be on their social media channels as well as blog comments. Secondly those bloggers writing interesting copy and those able to deliver what they say they will do. Domain Authority is also important as it measures the authority a blog has.

How to pitch

When you decide to bite the bullet and pitch a potential collaboration to a PR or brand ensure that you are prepared. Do your research and it will help you stand out from the vast amount of pitches they receive every day from bloggers.

Firstly, look on the brands website as often the press contact is listed at the bottom of the website this will give you the correct email to use.

Alternatively, Google the brand with phrases like 'who is the PR for XYZ?' and use LinkedIn to seek out the right contacts for a brand. This will help you track down the correct agency or person. Getting the right person is crucial otherwise your carefully thought out pitch will just disappear into cyberspace and may never reach the relevant person.

Once you have the email address you can then start crafting your proposal. Make it clear and to the point as you want it to be read. We suggest outlining how you would like to work with the brand in a paragraph. Then in a second paragraph detail what you will offer them; be it a blog post, social shares on your channels or banner advertising in your sidebar.

The tone should be friendly but professional. This is a working relationship and as such should follow set conventions, be polite, thank them for reading your email and use the right name and ensure you spell it correctly.

In your pitch include a link to your blog, and make it easy for the recipient to make connections about who you are. If the pitch is specific (which it should be) link to similar articles you have written as examples of your work. The easier you make it during an approach the more likely that you will be successful. Two links is probably enough but showcase what you can do. If you have a review that has lots of comments and was well received show the PR as it demonstrates what you can offer them if and when you work together.

Emma always adds her media pack to proposals and her media pack includes Emma's bio, her achievements and current and relevant statistics. It is a one page, visual document that is attached to emails. Emma's media pack was created using Canva which has templates for such things.

Lynn adds the first page from her more detailed PowerPoint media pack to pitch emails. This includes a summary of the blog, a picture of her, her logo and her key social statistics.

+

There are a few times when it is best to avoid sending your pitch.

Anecdotally we have been told that a Monday morning is not the best time as PR's and marketing departments are often in meetings and planning the week ahead, it is a busy time and emails may not get read fully and you may miss out just because it was bad timing.

Another cautionary tale is not to make blanket approaches to companies, if you are obviously sending out mass emails, do not expect much back in the way of replies.

Instead send carefully prepared individual pitches. Also, wait a while between approaching companies as if successful you could suddenly find yourself inundated with items to review and promote. Nothing sucks the life out of blogging when you have lots of reviews lined up – far from being fun it becomes a chore.

Once you have a contact at an agency ask or look at who their other clients are, and ask for your details to be shared with the people managing other accounts.

+

Nurture the relationship. PR's and brands are often busy and as we said it is a two-way relationship, we often have PR's asking if we can tweet something for them or support them on a campaign, we are happy to do this with agencies that we work with regularly. It is true that not all campaigns have huge budgets and a favour now will be remembered in the future.

Blogging has given us so many wonderful opportunities to travel and to try new products. We will also pitch when we are keen to try something. A few years ago Emma was after a new furniture set from a well-known brand. After some research, she could not find any evidence that they worked with bloggers. Undeterred she contacted the brand via Twitter and asked for an email contact. Over the course of a few emails Emma had struck a deal. She bought the furniture she wanted at cost price saving over £800. In exchange Emma blogged about her dining room makeover and promoted the brand. This worked well as a two-way partnership as Emma saved money and the brand received several blog posts and social media support.

Recently a 'TV in a card' appeared on Lynn's doorstep. It was a clever promotion addressed to a random name but at her address. It was a promotion for a new proposition, she took a chance and tweeted the PR agency mentioning the cool promotional device.

+

Lynn mentioned her website and that she would like to help with the promotion. The tweet was well received and she subsequently spoke to the agency on the phone. A sponsored post was agreed. The final touch was passing the contact over to Emma who also got the job, both netting the same generous fee.

Pitching develops with confidence but be prepared for many knock backs too. You could write a fantastic pitch but the timing is not right for the brand, they may have spent their budgets or they may be focussing on another campaign. Therefore, don't take a no as personal rejection, it could easily be just a case of 'not right now' but your name and blog may be remembered and something may come from it in the future.

Another tip is to pick up the phone and ring an agency. Agencies ring Lynn and Emma frequently to discuss campaigns and they both find this helpful as having a chat is good for getting to know individuals and once you know someone personally you seem to be remembered more.

However when pitching or being approached there will be times that the promised sponsored post or review item just does not materialise. Sometimes the emails just abruptly stop and the PR disappears or no longer replies.

This can feel like rejection but at times, budgets change, a PR changes jobs, the agency loses a contract or even a better proposition comes along. On these occasions it can be frustrating but our advice is to remain professional and just let it go. A tip is not to promise your children an event or product until you have it in hand no matter how likely it looked.

Pitching is a skill to be honed and we hope that this chapter has given you the confidence to sell yourself in this way. If you have a trusted blogger friend, ask them to read your pitch and give their feedback on it. Once you have had success with a pitch you know it works and then we suggest just tweaking it for the occasion.

+

Chapter 11 - How to Make Money from Your Blog

We get asked often how we earn money from blogging? It's a huge mystery to the world what we do and how it can be monetised. Non-bloggers are always really interested to discover all the different things we do. Commercially minded friends are always intrigued to understand this new phenomenon and how much money can be earned from a brand-new industry.

Emma and Lynn feel so excited to part of a blossoming new industry. Blogging has been around for a few years now and Emma is one of the originals buts it's only in recent years that brands have started to switch on to blogger outreach/collaborations. The bigger PR companies now have blogger outreach Execs and even outreach departments. PR Manager and Execs are often open and honest with us about brands. Some have embraced the new form of influential advertising media and others haven't.

+

Despite bloggers often being a one-man / one-woman operation we have an incredible amount of influence for one person. We might have a social media reach of 10,000 which in terms of corporate numbers is not huge, but when you then look at engagement, i.e. how many people like, comment, read our posts, we might have an engagement statistic of maybe 5,000, so we suddenly become an incredibly influential form of marketing.

Bloggers speak from the heart, we tell the truth, we are honest about our lives and our readers are interested in what we have to say. It then follows that if we adore a product and recommend it then our readers may well buy it. We are an extremely influential form of media so we should be paid for it!

Back to the nuts and bolts, we will go through each of the ways income can be generated from your blog. We also write this with an understanding of other bloggers and how they earn their money as we bloggers all have very different revenue splits.

Sponsored posts

A sponsored post is a blog post where you write about a chosen subject and drop in the name of a brand. Sometimes it might be obvious and sometimes it might be quite subtle. Our favourite sponsored posts are the ones where the blogger is open and obvious about the brand but is sharing something with you that is so relevant to their own blog brand.

Sponsored posts can be lucrative, but are very rare in the early days when you are lacking in content and social numbers. In the early days we suggest applying for opportunities shared in the Facebook groups or networks suggested later in chapter 7, to help you gain confidence.

The fee for sponsored posts will vary hugely from one brand to the next. We have been offered anything from £100 to £500 for collaborations. The standard rate we charge has grown over time.

+

A sponsored post can be about anything from a product to a service to a new website. We urge you to only take sponsored posts for brands that are relevant to your niche and that you can write about with authenticity and passion. Lynn's niche is personal finance and getting the most value for your hard-earned pounds so it would be wrong for her to write about pay day loans which are possibly the worst value products out there that take advantage of people in desperate financial situations. Readers would lose their faith in her. Pick and choose your brands wisely.

Be upfront with the brand/PR agency about what your fee will include. Will it include a do follow or no follow link? How much social media promotion will be included? Are there certain words they want included in the title, what key word would they like you to use? Agree timelines and check if they would like to review a draft before it is published.

The fee you might charge depends on a few things, take the following into consideration:

1) Research the brand. Are they a big brand with deep pockets for their marketing budget? Is it a big new proposition or product launch? If yes, go higher
2) Are you dealing direct with a brand or via a PR agency? Go higher if dealing direct with a brand.

3) Is the product you are promoting high value? If the client makes a £200 profit from each new customer you send, they can afford to pay you a higher fee
4) Have they sent you an individual/unique email specific to you and your blog. I.e. composed rather than copied and pasted? If so they are interested in you and your blog so go higher
5) How did they find you, was it a recommendation? If it was a recommendation by another blogger find out what the other blogger was paid.
6) Send them a media pack including all key statistics.

Affiliate earnings

Affiliate revenue is a fee earned for every new customer signed up to a product or service or a spend from a customer that you have driven to a website. Where sponsored posts are one-off fees, affiliate revenue is ongoing. The more traffic and readers you can drive to your post the more potential ongoing revenue you can earn.

Some affiliate partners will offer small commissions, and some offer big. You need to work out the sweet spot for you on this revenue that will work and generate earnings. Emma and Lynn have many brilliant blogger friends who swear by affiliate revenue and will do very few or no sponsored posts as they have the faith in their site traffic and the clicks from readers who then go to purchase a recommended product.

A big part of the key to affiliate success is traffic. The more readers you get to your website the more chances they will click on the link and purchase what you are recommending.

Examples of affiliate models

There are some big affiliate partner sites like Affiliate window and Skimlinks where you can join them and they act as an intermediary between you and retailers. They will pay your commission earned from the retailer less a cut. However, this is good practise as you don't have to spend all the effort working out the best person to speak to at each brand. Get signed up to these.

+

There are also direct relationships that can be set up. Amazon is a classic example, so every product you mention you could use an Amazon link and if the reader buys it (or anything else during that visit) you will earn a commission. You can see how these earnings can ramp up when your traffic hits high levels.

There might also be relationships with niche brands that have direct referral schemes where you have a relationship working together. For example, TopCashback, if we include a refer-a-friend link we earn a commission. Or if we work with a mystery shopping company we are passed a referral fee for each reader who signs up.

There are so many different referral schemes and if you can track the traffic to a purchase then a commission can be paid.

The best thing about affiliate earning is that it is passive, i.e. the money continues to roll in from your web posts whatever you are doing. A skillfully search engine optimised post will draw in traffic to your site on a continuing basis and if these posts include affiliate links, the earnings will follow.

Emma Drew Info gives the following advice on affiliate marketing:

I have blog posts from 5 years ago that are still earning me money on a daily basis. My top tip would be to only affiliate for products or services that you know and trust. Your readers come to your blog to hear from you, so they want to know what products and services actually benefit you. Not only does it keep you loyal to your readers, you are likely to earn more money by genuinely promoting products rather than linking to everything.

Writing for other publications or ghost writing

We know many bloggers make a great income out of this stream. Firstly, there is writing in your name for other publications. This might be for another website or for the press. If you are an expert in your field the publication will be keen to use your name and you can charge more the bigger your brand and blog becomes.

You can also get paid for ghost writing which is writing content that someone one else will put their name to. Brands will pay for great writing for their websites often if they like your style but want the writing to appear like it's directly from them.

Public speaking and media

When you write a blog on a niche subject, you are perfect for related public speaking and media appearances.

Emma has done a lot of this kind of work. She has written for years about hip dysplasia and has appeared on TV several times discussing the subject, its complications and the effect on her and Erin's life. She has appeared on many TV programmes from Good Morning Britain, ITN Lunchtime news, Channel Four News to BBC Breakfast and Radio shows.

Journalists may want to feature you in stories and use you as a case study. These opportunities are sometimes paid. And of course, you can pitch to newspapers and magazines and write in your own name. Emma has also done this in the past and was published in the Daily Mail after buying her daughters prom dress from China and it being a disaster!

Experts on a subject may also be asked to sit on panels in seminars and presentations offering their view point. Emma sat on the panel about blogger pay at the 2016 UK Money Blogger personal finance awards.

+

Prior to this Emma has spoken or chaired sessions at Britmums Live, Tots100 Blog Camp and Funfest. The bigger the events, the more you will be paid. Even if it's not paid it will increase your authority and demonstrate your power and influence and this in turn can build your brand.

Sell products

If you have spent some time building a brand with a large audience it's a great time to sell products. You have a readymade audience in your social media, contacts, email database and website traffic so you could make money from selling the right products.

Do you feature beautiful lifestyle items on Instagram that you get a lot of engagement from? Maybe you can sell these items. This can be set up using an affiliate model so you don't even have to hold the stock. Just make your site look slick and you can point people towards the sales website to make the actual purchase.

+

What can you do to monetise your blog? Use this page to make notes

+

Chapter 12 - How to Negotiate and Seal the Deal

Negotiation is a key skill for business and life. Learn and master this skill in the blogging world. It's not something that is ever taught in school and is something that many people are uncomfortable with, a bit like money management in both ways!

Lynn's background helps hugely here. Particularly at EE where she attended a week-long course on the subject of commercial negotiation.

The basics to negotiating can be explained by a few points

1) If you don't ask you don't get
2) There is nothing to feel uncomfortable about, just ask, it's business
3) Every extra pound you negotiate is extra money in your pocket
4) Everything is negotiable
5) What's the worst that can happen?
6) Fake it until you make it

Let's start with a real-life example of a great negotiation situation. Buying a car is great example to consider. Here is how Lynn would buy and negotiate a significant purchase:

1) Start with research to work out what cars you should consider. Investigate type, brand, safety, price range

+

2) Shortlist three different brands and visit their showrooms
3) Test drive three cars
4) You are likely to know your favourite after that
5) The best timing is to aim to purchase a car at the end of the dealerships quarter when they are keen for sales
6) Then you negotiate
7) Sales person says the list price is £10,000
8) Say you have £7,000 cash (cash is useful negotiating tactic to offer, cash is always preferred to credit)
9) State that you are in no rush for the car
10) Say that you are not fussed on the colour
11) The sales person drops their offer to £9,000
12) You counter offer £7,335 (a good tactic is to offer unrounded amounts, it's a psychological trick)
13) You walk away, so you are too far from each other
14) The sales person will call you after 24 hours. They are keen for the sale as it's the end of the quarter and they are working hard for their commission bonus. They have spoken to their Manager and they can drop to £8,250
15) You say you'll think about it
16) After another 24 hours, the sales person checks in again. They can miraculously drop to £7,900
17) You accept this price, as this was a great negotiation where you worked hard and got £2,100 knocked off the initial asking price
18) When it comes to payment and collection time a few days later you ask at the last minute for extras, such

as a free tank of petrol or mud mats for all the flooring. Keep asking for extras and be persistent. As soon as you sign on the dotted line and hand over the cash you won't be able to negotiate anything further.

Blogger Rates

Negotiating for any kind of blogging work is a very similar game. Sometimes it is easier to think of negotiating as a game and to have some fun with it. Remember, if you don't ask you don't get.

The difference with negotiating a blogging fee is that you are the sales person. You are selling your blog, your social media channels and you are selling yourself to the brand. So be bold and brave, big yourself up.

The other things to be aware of is that very few people are skilled negotiators so they might not know how to play the game. But use this to your advantage, this is a great time where you can go in high on your quote and it might just be accepted.

Here is how we would negotiate a blogger rate with a PR company in a perfect world:

1) An energy company has launched a new proposition. It's something different and you have a great idea for a pitch where you can naturally drop in the product and brand name and it fits in with your brand niche

2) You already have a relationship with the PR agency so you send them an initial email with the perfect pitch (see the pitching chapter 10). Your personality comes across and you know it's a great idea so it's a perfect pitch. Give them your latest social statistics.

3) The agency replies and says they love the idea, they are indeed doing blogger outreach and they ask what your sponsored post rate is?

4) This is a great response to a pitch and it is most likely a yes as you can agree the commercials

5) If it's a big brand with deep pockets, reference chapter 11 - how to make money from your blog, why not go in high. What's the worst that can happen? They could say no; well you can deal with that

6) Go in at £500, and say this will include social sharing on Facebook, Twitter and any other channel they see relevant

7) Wait to see what they come back with

8) If you hear nothing, pick up the phone and ask if the rate was acceptable.

9) Or send a chaser email after a few days of not hearing anything

10) Chase until you get a response. If that is "sorry your fee is too much", reply with OK and suggest a 20% discount and work down until you can reach somewhere that is comfortable for both sides

Lynn has recently negotiated a deal where she offered to do a sponsored post for £400, including social media sharing. They immediately called her telling her that the rates were too expensive and that it was way higher than the other bloggers had quoted. Lynn offered to reduce her rate by 20% and went down to £320. They replied by email this time saying that was still too high and that she need to justify the high rates. She replied saying she would drop to £200, her final offer and explained all the benefits of working with her. She included a few recent branded projects to show her value. At this point the job fee was accepted and the post agreed. With negotiating you have to accept that you cannot win them all.

Both Emma and Lynn have experienced some huge wins where they have been asked to quote, said £400 and it has been accepted with no questions. They have also been approached to do some work with the last line saying payment would be £500. They jump at those opportunities!

Negotiate other factors

It's not just money that you can negotiate. Think about the factors below when discussing opportunities with brands or PR agencies.

1) Is it an event where attendance will be a valuable experience? Sometimes the experience alone it worth great money

+

2) Will travel expenses be covered?

3) Will there be cross promotion of brands on social media channels or a mention on their brand website (great for back-link power)

4) Are there valuable free products included that you would have bought anyway?

5) Is there a promise of an ongoing relationship? Maybe it is a brand with potential and doing a free job to help them out now will mean they will help you in the future?

As with pricing there is no science to negotiation. You just have to go with it and be brave. You will learn so much over the course of a year or so running your blog. Go with your gut if you think the brand or PR agency has money to spend, and go in high. Be prepared to negotiate. Every extra pound is more money in your pocket and more profit for your blog.

+

Chapter 13 - Collaborations and How They Can Benefit You

Collaborations raise many questions, not least about the benefits of working with other bloggers. In this chapter, we want to encourage bloggers to build relationships and look at working collaboratively. There are many ways to work with others and the benefits are immense.

Blogging can be seen as a solitary business, with the image of bloggers sitting at their laptops in their own homes and not really talking to anyone else. Yet the most successful bloggers do work with others forging working relationships and friendships across the country and in some cases across the globe. Successful bloggers don't see themselves in competition with fellow bloggers. Although they chase the same brand opportunities they realise that sharing contacts and sharing ideas can only be a good thing.

Collaborations can take many forms from running linkys (a blog post where lots of bloggers can share a related blog post and read and comment on lots of others), running blogs together and a whole host of other ways to make money as a group or partnership. This is probably a great place to explain just how this book came together as a joint venture.

Emma and Lynn had very briefly connected in a Facebook group and were both attending the UK Money Bloggers conference. Emma was feeling brave and flying solo attending a conference with bloggers that she didn't really know that well. Emma sought out Lynn to meet in person. Within a few minutes of meeting they knew that they were coming from the same place. They complemented each other's skills set, they chatted and their minds started whirring!

Emma was speaking at the conference and the panel had a very heated discussion on money and working with brands in general and another blogger in the room suggested that a book should be written about the subject being discussed. The seed was planted and the very next day Emma contacted Lynn to see whether she was open to a collaboration, only to find out she had been thinking the same. They had several chats and met in person at an event they were both invited too. It was then full steam ahead to write Blogging Your Way To Riches.

Together Emma and Lynn make a great team with different strengths and they made this happen. Lynn for example is brilliant at setting deadlines and taking the lead on turning the dream into a reality. She worked efficiently at getting contracts drawn up and the practical side of self-publishing a book.

Emma sourced the clothes for the photoshoot and took on some of the more creative tasks including the cover of the book. If we share that we have conceived the idea of the book, have written it, published and promoted it ourselves, on a budget, in just three months many would probably not believe that is achievable but here it is and we have. Collaborations are game changers!

Why bloggers benefit from informal collaborative working

Primarily it is fun to work with others, as we have already said self-employment can be lonely and isolating. Just take a few minutes to look at some of the UK's most high profile and popular bloggers and you will see evidence of working together. Working together brings out the social. Blogging is social, blogging is about making connections and if you can do this it will grow your blog and readers. Many bloggers are incredibly supportive of other bloggers and by building your own tribe or network you can support each other.

A tribe of likeminded bloggers can be an informal way of collaborating, you can agree to share each other's posts and it will undoubtedly have a positive impact on your traffic. No-one wants to write a post only to see it have little reach and that only your mum and best friend reads.

Informal collaborations also allow for sharing opportunities. We don't mean open-up your book of contacts and give them all away but one way we have had success is that if we are working on a campaign we will suggest other bloggers it may suit. They reciprocate in the same way and this helps us all to develop new contacts and opportunities.

Informal collaborating can be inspiring and can save you time. Having people to bounce ideas off and share good practice with is empowering. Emma has many bloggers that she has now known for years and will use them as a sounding board for new ideas. We also look out for each other if we see a campaign that they would be great for. There are lots of bloggers working like this and it helps you feel connected to the blogging community and makes the whole thing feel like fun. Collaborating like this is also a smart time saver, when you are pitching for work or searching out opportunities you are not actually earning money. By introducing brands to your 'tribe' you are saving yourself time.

Molly Forbes, editor of Roost explains the benefits of running a blog collaboratively.

There are lots of advantages of working collaboratively on a blog, for me, the number one has to be working as part of a team with inspiring and creative people. Blogging can sometimes be quite an isolating job, although we're part of a thriving and chatty community, the actual act of working is done on our own, often from home. To be part of a team and be able to bounce ideas around and draw on our own individual strengths is a huge bonus.

The other plus is that we have a wider combined reach because we all have our own individual followers that we can bring to the platform. This is often a big draw for brands and means that the site took off far quicker than if we were starting out as a solo new blogger.

How Bloggers Can Collaborate

Linkys

Running linkys together is a great way to start collaborating with other like-minded bloggers. Linkys work by creating a theme and inviting other bloggers to link up their posts on the same theme.

One example is Five Fabulously Frugal Things which is co-hosted by Emma, Cass from Frugal Family and Becky from Family Budgeting. Each Friday all three hosts publish a post listing five ways that they have saved money during the week. They invite others to link up and this is developing a community of thrifty bloggers. The posts are shared, commented on and promoted.

The benefit for the group hosting the linky is growing authority in an area, where the group are key players in the thrifty blogging circles. Secondly each member of the linky will grow their audience and traffic by being part of a community. Setting up collaborative linky is also a time saving approach, but as the linky becomes popular it becomes very time consuming. All posts need to be commented and shared on Twitter. The more you do this the more successful the linky becomes but this takes time. Sharing the responsibility for a linky ensures that it runs smoothly, and it also allows co-hosts a week off every now and then without disrupting people's expectations. Finally, it helps to provide more backlinks to your blog which improve your social metrics and Domain Authority which in turn can bring more paid brand opportunities.

Collaborative Blog

There are a growing number of collaborative blogs and this seems to work particularly well within niche topics. Each person in the collaboration has a different role and how you set this up would be a personal choice. Molly Forbes is Editor of the successful collaborative blog Roost. While Molly retains control, there are regular contributors that write a specific theme or section of the blog. Other collaborative blogs include Space in your Case where four bloggers came together to launch a travel blog. Working like this means that responsibility is shared. These collaborative blogs are often run as a second blog and therefore it is an efficient way of working. As an individual you may not have enough content to write several times a week, but by doing a post each a week, it becomes do-able. It then ensures the collaborative blog runs to schedule.

Collaborative Posts on Blogs

There are a few different options here. You might write a guest post on another blogger's site and they might then return the favour. This helps create content and you may gain a new audience after they read your content elsewhere. You also benefit from back links to each other's sites.

There are 'crowd sourced' posts, where you write about a subject area and collect quotes from other bloggers or link to other related content. Referral traffic can be significant if the right website is directing traffic your way. Lynn has collaborated several times on YouTube and blog content with Wacey Style. These collaborations have been lots of fun, making videos about capsule wardrobes, bargain make up and changing up a boring wardrobe.

If making money important to you (let's face it, it is important to many of us) then collaborations can raise your profile and bring more opportunities to your door. This book is a collaborative idea and a spin off from our own blogs. Other bloggers are collaborating and setting up joint ventures developed from their blogs. Hannah from Budding Smiles has recently set up an online shop Apples and Pips and sells products from other bloggers, such as handmade leggings from Lamb and Bear.

Elsewhere bloggers are setting up eBooks, courses and social media businesses together. Collaborating really can elevate your blog, reputation and reach.

+

How can you collaborate with others? List bloggers you can approach to work.

+

Chapter 14 - Search Engine Optimisation (SEO) Demystified for Success

Search Engine Optimisation (SEO) is super important in the website world. You could have the most attractive website with all the bells and whistles but if no one can find it what's the point? Why invest all the time in creating a masterpiece of incredible writing in a brilliant format if no-one reads it?

SEO is most closely associated with Google as most people use Google as their search engine of choice. Think of Google as the ultimate dictionary or index of content on the internet. But it's not as simple an alphabetical listing of content, oh no! There is a hugely complex mathematical algorithm that sits behind it, which constantly changes the order of websites listed for search terms.

But do not fear, it's a subject that can be cracked by following a few rules. It's not complicated, we mastered it, and it is something you can do yourself. We have both learnt the basics and maintain good SEO principles with every piece of content we write.

Mrs Mummypenny's SEO mistakes

When Lynn first created Mrs Mummypenny she made a huge mistake, and did not focus on SEO. Reflecting back, it was a significant mistake as the process of repairing it is extremely time-consuming. The phrase 'get it right first time' is so relevant here. Lynn relied on social media sharing to get the traffic to her site. This worked well and was always a pretty consistent way to get a good number of hits to the site. But as time went on Lynn started talking to other bloggers, and realised that she was missing out on a huge opportunity of thousands of extra website views per month.

Comparing traffic numbers with other bloggers can be good and bad.

Good because it can make you realise you might be doing something wrong so you can learn new ways to make your site more searchable. But it can also be bad as you get disheartened about the higher amount of traffic to another site and it might feel unachievable. Never feel like this. Site traffic is important but not the most important thing in the world. Most important is your writing and the relationship you have with your readers, however they find you. Just think of SEO as a great way to get more readers to find your website.

+

Also people embellish and exaggerate their traffic numbers to sound bigger than they are. It's a difficult thing to check, there are many sites that will give you traffic. You can set up Google Analytics to get accurate figures for your traffic, but external parties cannot check your sites traffic perfectly. Also, there are plenty of traffic related terms linked to your site. Are you quoting monthly unique users, or monthly page views? Are you quoting bounce rate (the higher the ratio of page views to user the lower the bounce rate)? Be careful and don't believe everything you hear.

Basics of SEO

The key to SEO is appearing on the first page when someone searches for certain words or sentences in Google, which is called ranking high in SEO terminology. This term will be searched potentially thousands of times in the UK and the world and you want people to then click on the link to your website.

+

Try typing a search term into Google that you want your website to be known for. A term that Lynn would love to rank highly for is 'Personal Finance Expert in UK'. When this is typed into Google there is a list of websites. You will often get a paid listing first, then it flows into unpaid listings. The list contains a few surprises with a few bloggers making it to page one, it's the top three-five that matters and will probably get 80% of the traffic.

1) First on the list is Quidco, a cashback company, which has written a post about their Twitter list of favourite experts

2) Second is Money Saving Expert, Martin Lewis who started his own blog and made it big, really big! Money Saving Expert is now a big organisation with many people to work on SEO

3) Third is Sarah Pennells, a very reputable personal finance expert, one of the first Lynn came across and followed years ago

4) Fourth is a site selling insurance which has written their list of favourite podcasts

5) Fifth is a post from a wonderful blogger and friend Money Nuggets writing about her top personal financial experts.

The aim is to get into the top five un-paid for positions for as many search terms as possible. This will drive a lot of traffic to your site. Reflect back to chapter 11 and how to make money from your blog. Traffic means more readers. More readers mean they are more likely to click through affiliate links on your site. Emma has mastered SEO well for hip dysplasia and frequently ranks highly for searches related to hip dysplasia. Her aim now is to achieve the same for other key terms and especially money saving terminology.

Examples of people who are great at SEO

There are some great SEO experts within the UK Money Bloggers circle and we have learnt tips from them over the past year. One of the best is Andy Webb who runs the UK Money Bloggers group, website and his own site Be Clever With Your Cash. He has written about some quirky but popular money saving hacks and consistently appears at the top of the Google search pages for these terms.

Andy wrote an article titled called 'Cash Hacks – Great trick to get an NUS student discount card even when you're not a student'. Enter any type of NUS related search term into Google and his site pops up on page one, really near the top, normally position two or three. This is a very clever piece of writing, SEO and affiliate marketing laced together. It's a brilliantly written piece of content.

Andy writes in a simple and clear way, explaining the money saving hack, how it could save you money and how to do it. The post is laced with affiliate links to things you need to sign up to take advantage of the hack, so the traffic flowing through his site makes him money.

So how did he do it? Basically, his post is perfectly optimised for search engines.

1) The title contains key words that people may be searching for – NUS student discount card being the main words
2) The post reads well, so you are likely to read from beginning to end
3) It has a structure, with titles
4) The grammar is great with no spelling mistakes
5) The writing style is relaxed and humorous
6) Andy keeps the post updated regularly with new links. Great for Google juice

+

7) It includes simple and effective graphic as the featured image containing his website name and the key words.
8) He has added a YouTube link chatting through the cash hack
9) He replies to every comment and engages with readers

Take a look at the article for yourself and see what you think.

However Andy himself points out that you can't rely on Google search rankings to always continue delivering great traffic. There is always the risk that someone else will come along and write a post that ranks higher in future searches.

Yoast - A WordPress Plugin to help you out

About six months ago Lynn discovered the Yoast plug-in for WordPress. A tad embarrassing that it took so long to discover this, but there you go. The last year has been the most learning Lynn has done since she was studying for her accountancy exams.

All the steps described in Andy's perfect SEO post are detailed in Yoast and it helps you to create great SEO posts yourself. Write your post and then go to the Yoast section at the bottom of your post and it will give you a traffic light system for all the things you need to change and improve to make the post more optimised. It will advise on things like title, keyword, meta description, slug, ALT attributes for images, word count, paragraph titles and structure. It will flag red if it's not good enough and changes to green when you repair it.

This plugin literally changed our SEO lives when we started using it. We both saw an immediate jump in traffic. After a while of using the plugin your writing style tends to change and as you write the post you will start to write it as a perfect SEO post. You will use headers and shorter paragraphs. You will drop in the key word a few times through the content. Soon you learn the skill and it becomes a habit. The day we get a green light when first checking Yoast will be a good day.

Other SEO Pointers that are great for Google Juice

Through our many SEO discussions (yes we have both sat at dinner with fellow bloggers discussing Google search rankings!) there are many top tips we can share. Here are a few more:

+

- Do your key word research and choose keywords that are relevant to your post and searchable
- Be clever with your title. Use Google to help. Type in your keyword and see what titles are thrown up below the search box
- Add new content to your site consistently. It could be daily or weekly but keep it consistent.
- Go back and improve SEO on older posts, and focus on those with higher traffic first. Mrs Mummypenny has some posts with accidental high traffic, i.e. She made no effort on SEO but they naturally get a lot of traffic every day. These posts should be the first ones to updates for SEO and add in affiliate links for monetisation
- Update old posts with new links or press news
- When writing new content link back to your previous blog posts. It bounces traffic around your site and keeps people reading your content for longer
- Share you posts on Google+. It helps with SEO rankings as it's Google's social media platform

Chapter 15 - How to Comply with Regulations when Blogging

When you are putting information out into the universe you cannot do and say anything you like. There are many guidelines and regulations you need to follow and we thought it prudent to share some of the most important things you need to get right when earning money from blogging. These are non-negotiables and you must comply. There are many areas still under consideration in the blogging world. It is still a very new industry and new regulations could come in at any time. Therefore, we advise you to keep up to date with your knowledge in these areas by joining blogging groups and discussing them with your network.

Self Employed Status with Inland Revenue

Once you earn even £1 from blogging you will need to set yourself up as self-employed. The process can be done online and is relatively straight forward. You will be responsible for submitting your tax return each year and paying any tax due. There is a personal allowance and for many bloggers you may not reach the threshold required to pay tax and that is perfectly acceptable. A simple Google search will tell you the current tax threshold, for the tax year 2015/16 it is £10,600.

+

Even if you earn less than this amount, you do still have to register and declare your earnings and then you will be told you don't owe any tax. You can register as self-employed alongside having paid employment. The two will marry up at the tax office and be reflected in your tax return. Both Emma and Lynn employ an accountant to oversee this and it can cost just a few hundred pounds for an accountant to set you up and do your accounts each year providing, you keep the records.

For more advice visit the www.gov.uk website.

Sole Trader or Limited Company?

When registering as self-employed you can set up as sole trader or a limited company. There are differences between the two and for many bloggers a sole trader is enough but if you are planning blogging domination and have a large turnover then a limited company will be a better option from a tax consideration. The difference is a limited company is its own legal identity, so as a shareholder your liability is limited. As a sole trader, there is little distinction between you and the business. Any business debts become your debts and your personal assets - including your house - are not protected.

+

Track your income and outgoings

A simple Excel spreadsheet is enough to record all income from blogging, including all cash and vouchers paid to you for your blogging work. On another spreadsheet list all your outgoings which can be claimed as expenses. This will include but is not limited to mobile phone costs, broadband fees, PayPal fees, postage and stationery costs, food when at events, travel costs including hotel stays due to attending events and petrol.

If you work from home, you can also offset a proportion of your energy and water bills against your business income. You can also include equipment you buy for the sole purpose of blogging, Emma's new Canon G7X would be an example as it has been bought for blogging. These costs will all be offset against your income when completing your tax return. Keeping receipts is essential. If the HMRC decide to investigate your business they can ask for receipts for the previous seven years to prove your income and outgoings.

Advertising Standards Agency (ASA) Disclosure

Disclosure is governed by the Advertising Standards Agency (ASA) and it tells bloggers that you cannot be misleading about a product and that you need to make it clear to your audience where you are working with a brand on either paid posts or reviews.

To comply with these requirements bloggers should add a disclosure at the top or bottom of a post. Bloggers may include #ad or #spon in the post title. Emma makes the relationship explicit in the post saying things like 'Brand X gave me complimentary tickets for Y'. The ASA has not prescribed the wording bloggers must use – rather the requirement is that the disclosure and working relationship needs to be declared somewhere. The disclosure is needed on social media channels in addition to your blog. Bear this in mind with YouTube, Twitter and Instagram too. We suggest always discussing how the brand would like the collaboration to be worded when agreeing the details of the post and / or relationship.

Competition Regulations

Competition regulations governs the rules around running competitions on your blog and on your social media channels. Many bloggers run competitions as it can be a beneficial way to grow your social media audience. It is also fantastic to be able to reward your audience with fun competitions. Bloggers host all types of competitions and in the past Emma has given away an iPhone 6, a spa break and beauty products.

Bloggers work hard to source prizes from brands to promote the competitions but as a blogger you must have terms and conditions set out. When hosting a competition, there must be a clear end time and date. The prize must be described and everyone should be able to enter if they chose to. To get a full understanding of running competitions we recommend looking at Super Lucky Me where comping expert Di Coke can guide bloggers through setting up a blog giveaway.

Images

You must be aware of image theft. As a blogger, you can't just lift any image you want to include on your blog as this is theft. You cannot just Google an image and use it. The same is true for music on YouTube. Not to worry, as there are a plethora of sites that have stock images, many of which are free to use. When collaborating with a brand it is always better to take and use your own images as this shows that you have used and tried the product. If you are unable to use your own the brand will probably be able to send you asset shots that you can use. Another option is asking other bloggers if they have an image you can use, it is good blogging etiquette to credit the photograph with a link back to the blogger's site.

Copyright laws

These laws apply to text and blog posts. You cannot lift another person's work or plagiarise it on your own blog. There are likely to be many similar blogs and an idea is not copyrightable but having duplicate content can be a problem for bloggers. Text is intellectual property and you cannot take this from someone else as it is theft.

Trademarks

In addition to copyrights bloggers need to be aware of trademarks. Trademarks and copyrights protect different types of intellectual property. A trademark typically protects brand names and logos used on goods and services. Copyright protects an original artistic or literary work. Be aware when using images and brand names that you are using the correct versions. You can also trademark your own business name when it grows to a significant business. This is done by registering your name with the Intellectual Property Office which will protect the use of your name in the UK. This is only suitable for blogs set up as a limited company.

Privacy

Privacy is important and as a blogger you cannot capture data on anyone and sell it on or pass it on without prior consent. This includes when running competitions or when collecting email addresses of subscribers. In the same way if you have a newsletter you must have an opt out clause so when someone chooses not to subscribe to your service anymore they can remove their details.

Libel laws

Think before you write as libel laws protect individuals and brands. You can't say whatever you like about people unless you are prepared to be sued. Libel laws do not just apply to national newspapers they apply to everyone and once you have written something in haste online you will not be able to withdraw it easily. Think before you write. When we see bloggers being personal online, we cringe. It is not professional but in the main it could be seen as libel and land you in serious trouble. Remember your brand and remember to play nicely!

Google guidelines

Google is not the law but it does have guidelines on selling links. When you link out of your blog the natural link is a follow link. A follow link passes authority between your blog and the site you are linking to. Google counts the links and the authority of every link and if the link has been paid for, Google believes that this will skew the natural balance of their ranking system. Therefore they want links to be made 'no follow' if they are paid for links. You can do this by adding some HTML code or using a plugin if on WordPress.

+

If Google decide that you have been paid for links and they are follow links they will contact you via your Google dashboard and tell you to change them. As a penalty they can remove you from the search engine findings. This could have a detrimental effect on your traffic sources. You can resubmit your blog once it is 'clean' and be reinstated. A natural question is why some agencies want you to use a follow link despite it being paid for. The simple answer is that they want the link juice, the authority and to rank higher in Google, whereas Google want the results to be organic.

These guidelines, laws and regulations are vital to know and understand as mistakes could be costly and leave a blogger open to being sued or their reputation and authority being questioned. It is the responsibility of every blogger to ensure that they are complying with the laws, rules and guidelines.

Chapter 16 - What Can I Outsource to Save Time and Make Blogging Easier

Creating a successful blog and brand is a time-consuming task. You could spend 18 hours a day perfecting the craft every day and still not have the time to do everything. In the early days you do have to do most stuff yourself, possibly hating some of it, but when earning very little income you have no choice.

Go back to the basics was the advice from one of Lynn's business mentors. In the early days make as much money as you can and spend as little money as possible.

Every penny should only be spent on meaningful things or services that will create value for your business, and more value than they cost. Return on income is a great business calculation which one would always use in the business world when assessing the cost of things. Compare the cost of something to the income it will provide in a certain time period.

At the beginning of Mrs Mummypenny the big thing that Lynn paid for was the logo. Lynn has no creative design skills whatsoever. A friend helped out and designed the logo for use on website, social media and all communication to come from Mrs Mummypenny. Lynn was very grateful for the professional design from day one of the blog.

Be careful with what you choose to outsource in the early days. Here is our recommendation for what to outsource when income is low and you need to get your business looking slick and professional.

The Early 'Tighter' Days

Logo Design

If you have no graphic design skills like both of us, there are a few bargain options for logo design. You could give Fiver a try and pay £5 for a logo that will be designed in 24 hours! OK it might not be that great. That logo will be in one file format, and you need several different formats for all your different social channels and printed materials and to get all those extra services it will cost more. If the logo is important to the professional look of the site, then maybe spend a little more and go with someone who has been recommended.

Website design

Neither Emma nor Lynn paid for web design in the early days. The WordPress set up is so intuitive that a relative technophobe, could set it up. It didn't look the best in the early days, the content was badly optimised but it didn't matter. Lynn could create content and learn the ropes. If this feels impossible and you want a great looking site from the early days, you need a web designer. We both recommend Hannah who blogs at Hi Baby Blog.

Finance - Accounting

This depends on your financial set-up. Lynn employed an accountant in September 2015 when she started running her blog on a full-time basis. Mrs Mummypenny was set up as a limited company from the beginning with the belief that this blog and brand was one day going to be +£100,000 turnover company. The accountant produces the annual accounts after being sent a spreadsheet of all income and expenses. Financial and tax advice is provided whenever it's needed all for a fee of £500 per year. A limited company is only advisable when you consider your business to have significant growth possibilities and you want to create a separate entity that protects your personal assets.

Most bloggers will be set up as a self-employed business. This can be done relatively easily by yourself. You just need clear records of all your income and expenses and you need to register your self-employed status with the Inland Revenue. You will need to do some research of your expenses, refer to chapter 15 for more tips on recording income and expenditure.

IT disaster person

Not a nice thing to think about, but you are probably not an IT disaster recovery person. Who has a clue what to do when faced with the blue screen of death? We all just call the IT support department. Welcome to the blogging world, where you don't have that convenient service anymore.

Back in September 2015, Lynn learnt this lesson the hard way. Her laptop was getting quite old and she should have been backing up everything and should have just bought a new laptop. Hindsight is a wonderful thing. Microsoft kept telling Lynn to add the Windows 10 update, she eventually gave into the prompts and did it. The result was one dead laptop. The update killed it, no recovery possible. 100% dead. PC World couldn't recover anything and neither could her IT expert friend, now Lynn's disaster recovery person.

+

Thankfully Lynn used Dropbox and it contained many of her documents, photos and videos, although not everything. Lynn complained to Microsoft and ended up getting £150 in compensation and £100 in Microsoft store credit. Another lesson there that you must always complain.

So please, please ensure that you have adequate IT protection and back everything up to a separate hard drive. Get some IT technical advice. Lynn's expert did other brilliant efficiency things like sorting out email accounts, only important emails from PR agencies and friends get through to a priority inbox, and most stuff ends up in clutter or junk.

These IT disasters do happen from time to time, Emma has been hacked a couple of times and while your first reaction might to cry and scream when you are faced with a screen informing you pirates have control of your site (yes, really) and random music is playing you need to stay calm. Often your first port of call is your web host as they can often rectify most things.

Emma is hosted with Evohosting and they have always provided brilliant support both on the phone and by emails. They took just a few hours to get control back of the blog and remove the hack. It was stressful for Emma but all in a day's work for the IT team who sorted it out. This is also what you pay your hosting for so ensure you speak to them before trying anything else.

Notice that in the early days it is essential or to look professional from the outside looking in. If you know someone who can help just ask, they can only say no, but will most likely say yes. Who knows they might be a contributor to an incredible successful blog one day and we would all like to associate with success, wouldn't we?

Outsourcing when you have income

We strongly believe that once you reach a certain level of income you tip into being able to afford more support. It's a time versus money debate. If you can earn £50 per hour, then it's worth you paying someone else £10-20 per hour to do other things. When you work by yourself you can spend so much time on admin tasks.

Lynn would suggest that at least 25% of her time was taken up with admin in the first year that could be farmed out. Just get to that comfortable point where you feel it's worth it to outsource. Also if you simply hate doing admin stuff it will always fall to the bottom of a to-do list and will never get done. But some admin stuff has to be done!

Here is our perfect world list of roles we either outsource already or intend to outsource soon.

Book-keeping

We both hate book-keeping, which is slightly ironic for Lynn as a qualified accountant. It's the receipts and the on-going process of keeping accurate records of money that has been spent. Lynn was not sensible and kept all the receipts stored in monthly envelopes, they were never transferred into a spreadsheet. A book-keeper has been employed to turn all these expenses into a spreadsheet. The book-keeper will get an envelope every month with expenses along with copies of bank statements on-going now and provide a monthly summary of profits. This can then easily be sent over to the Accountant for production of annual accounts. Expect to pay around £20 to £30 per hour for a book-keeper.

Virtual Assistant

Emma has a Virtual Assistant (VA) and we know a few other bloggers who also use them. A VA is perfect for any kind of admin tasks including the income and expenses recording that you might outsource to a book-keeper. The Virtual Assistant could manage your diary, keep track of deadlines, send out invoices, manage payments and keep track of late payments. They might proof read your posts, reply to emails, post on social media for you and make payments for you.

An incredible amount of admin stuff can be covered by the Virtual Assistant and they can work from their own location. Trust is a huge consideration here. Your assistant can end up being the most important cog in your busy business life and any mistakes made will reflect on you so make sure you employ the right person. Emma's Virtual Assistant is another school mum and they work both together and remotely, which works for them. When Emma has local events or meals to review she will often bring her VA as it helps her understand the work that she does plus it is nice to share the rewards of a successful blog.

Is there a mum who used to be a personal assistant (PA) in her previous life and needs some extra cash? We are both huge fans of using mum's and local people for any help with our businesses. We trust them, we are supporting fellow small business owners and we help out friends with an income. Expect to pay £10-£20 an hour for a VA.

Web design

Already mentioned, but this becomes more important as you grow in status as a blogger. Brands will look at your website and will want to see a professional design that's easy to navigate and read. When the time is right it's a great idea to invest some money in a slick and professional website. You can give them a wish list of everything that annoys you that would give you the perfect website and let them create for you. Or why not get a friend to critique it for you. A fresh pair of eyes is invaluable for things you might not have spotted yourself. Expect to pay from £100-£500 for a website redesign.

Legal/Accountant

As your business grows you are likely to have legal questions. A few recent ones from both of us concern trademarks, partnership agreements and shareholder agreements. Joining the Federation of Small Business is a great idea as for a fee of £130 year you get free legal advice and template document for tons of business situations. Legal advice will cost you £200 per hour so being a member is almost worth it just for the legal advice.

The advice on using an accountant has already been covered, but we recommend paying for accountancy as your business grows. You are less likely to be questioned about your operations if you pay for a professional to look after it for you. They know all the rules around tax, expenses and income so should do the job properly. As a guide you should expect to pay around £200-£300 for self-employed accounts and £500 for limited company accounts.

+

Agent

We are getting into a world where your income might be quite a bit higher. All the big vloggers have an agent. Agents act on your behalf, get work with media and brands and take a percentage of the fee. Your agent will work on behalf of other bloggers too and should be highly connected to the PR world of media, newspapers and brands. This can be a lucrative relationship and a good agent can be worth their weight in revenue.

Outsourcing is personal choice but try to match it to consistent earnings. A great rule to remember is that if you have the income, hate the task and can pay someone relatively cheaply to do it then outsource it.

Chapter 17- Longer Term Diversification and Making Even More Money

Once you are making regular money from your blog and you have built up your contacts you may consider taking your blog up a level.

Professional Blogger or Pro Blogger is a term that splits the blogging community like no other. For some bloggers this means that their blog is their sole source of income, they blog full time and make a full-time wage from blogging. We can see that some use this term to distinguish themselves from hobby bloggers but the argument that all bloggers should be professional renders the title a little lame!

Whether you call yourself a blogger, pro blogger or freelance writer depends on you and only you. You can decide what title you give yourself, but we find it helpful to think about how you want to describe yourself and what you put on your business cards!

Personally both Emma and Lynn describe themselves as bloggers, rather than writers. Lynn uses the term personal finance and lifestyle blogger which clearly identifies her niche. Emma tends to say that she is a blogger and editor as she works for Tots100 as a freelance editor.

Whatever you choose be proud of the term blogger and we believe that by using blogger as a title it will raise the profile of all bloggers. There has been a huge shift in understanding what a blogger does but as a new and growing industry not everyone yet understands the term and how bloggers make money.

When working freelance and making blogging your primary income, it is important to consider other income streams. While our blogs are an important stream of income we have both carved out other opportunities for additional income.

As a freelancer you can lose a regular client at any time and both Emma and Lynn have experienced this. While it is always disappointing when it happens, it is business and as such you need to pick yourself up and carry on. It helps if you know why the client no longer needs you. Emma was writing a regular weekly feature for over a year for an education recruitment website and was suddenly given a weeks' notice. This was because it's whole blog and social media effort was being outsourced. It was no reflection on her work but was disappointing nonetheless. It provides an example of the highs and lows of working for yourself.

Here is Emma's account of how she has diversified her income over the past two years:

In the months leading up to handing in my notice as a Head of Department teaching three days a week in a large comprehensive school I planned my transition. I was already earning money from blogging via sponsored posts but I knew that this alone was not going to be enough. I needed to sustain our standard of living and whilst I didn't need to earn the same as I had previously because I would have less childcare and fuel costs I still needed a regular reliable income. Once I handed in my notice I started actively looking for more paid opportunities.

To get me through that first exciting but financially challenging year I decided taking on GCSE exam marking and personal tutoring. Both helped bridge the gap as I adjusted to being self-employed full time. It was a good move but I only had to do it for one year and then I was able to drop the marking because it was boring! I had also set up my second blog Mums Savvy Savings, to create a second income stream from a different sector.

+

At this point I made a determined effort to focus Emma and 3 on education, health, empowerment while Mums Savvy Savings was obviously money related. Both are areas that I love and that I have always talked about. Although I am no longer teaching I am still committed to education and believe that parents have a fundamental role to play and I try to convey that in the blog. I have also always been a bargain hunter and like the satisfaction of stretching my pound further.

Having two blogs is challenging, and I use the same social media accounts as I couldn't manage two of everything but it still takes a lot of time to maintain two blogs. Whilst two blogs does mean a higher income it means that I am writing on both blogs three or four times a week. This is in addition to editing for others and blogger outreach.

In addition to the blogs I started looking at other ways I could make money as I wanted a portfolio career. I was very aware that if one income stream dropped off I would be hit financially.

When visiting Elance, a freelance site I saw the opportunity to write educational pieces for an educational recruitment agency. I pitched and was successful in my bid. They paid £30 for a post, and I delivered one post a week. Due to my qualifications the post required minimal research and I was able to cross link to my own blogs which helped with backlinks and traffic. This helped me gain confidence and kept me busy with a regular income. I started being more proactive searching out campaigns to get involved with. I emailed most of my contacts letting them know I was available and reminding them I was now blogging full time. In quiet times I still drop an email now and then reminding them about my blogs!

With my presence growing I was contacted to speak at various blogging conferences and while I am not always paid as a speaker these opportunities put me in front of audiences and brands and have generated commissions. I have also spoken at other events on topics that I am passionate about. Last year I spoke about Young Carers at their conference. This came about after getting involved in a campaign with Young Carers. It was wonderfully to add my voice to such a worthwhile cause.

＋

This year I branched out into blogger outreach and social media management. Both were goals I set myself and both have been realised. First up came the blogger outreach, I pitched because I was looking for revision aids for my daughter who was preparing for her GCSE's. I spoke with the founder and we agreed a review post. My contact was pleased with the results of the blog post and I then pitched him the idea of working with a set number of bloggers every month. He agreed and we moved on to discuss terms. The bloggers carry out a paid review and I recruit and manage the blog posts each month. I report back to him monthly. This is a nice regular client and each month I receive a set fee from him. It just demonstrates what can come from a small seed so always think big, continue to be commercial and upsell!

Once I had been running blogger outreach for a few months I started looking for another opportunity and it came via Facebook. A friend who runs her own business asked if anyone knew anything about getting someone to run your social media accounts. I quickly saw an opportunity, dropped her a message and after a chat I now run her Facebook and Twitter pages. Yet again this provides another income stream.

The combination make me a good monthly income and while I don't want to lose any clients I have things well spread because you never know when things will change. Diversification has been the key for me and this ensures that I have a regular income and I am not relying on a single source. It also provides me with room for more growth as I add more clients to my portfolio.

In this chapter, we share other ways that successful bloggers have diversified their income and built other revenues as off shoots from the blog. You can achieve the same and make the dream a reality.

Blogger Outreach

This is a natural step for experienced bloggers as they understand blogging and what is required. Blogger Outreach involves you working as the middle person between a brand and blogger, similar to a PR agency. Your role might include commissioning bloggers with the required profile for your client. You handle the contact and ensure the blogger understands the brief and the social media support required. You will chase up late posts and this is where blogger outreach becomes more time consuming as not everyone delivers as promised in the expected timeframe.

Once posts are written you collate them and record them in the format you have agreed with the client. Then the spreadsheet is passed to the client. The rates of pay vary hugely for blogger outreach depending on a number of variables including how many blogs are commissioned each month and the topic.

From speaking to other bloggers that run blogger outreach the rates vary from £25 per blog post to £100 per blog post. Finding clients for blogger outreach can be difficult so we suggest advertising the service on your media pack and also on your blog page under 'work with me'. These opportunities will not come from PR agencies as it's a service they offer clients but if you work directly with a new or small company it is worth mentioning that you could do blogger outreach for them.

Social Media Management

Social Media Management is another role where bloggers can develop their skills and expertise. Bloggers often use several social media channels to promote and grow their own audience therefore it is natural to then cross over and do this for clients. Be wary that it is not as easy as some might believe and when you are turning it into an income stream it is not just a case of tweeting something and popping up a Facebook status a few times a week.

You will need to understand the tone of the brand you are posting on behalf of. You will need to look into analytics and provide feedback to the client each month. The feedback will include growth in followers but also engagement which is even more important than the numbers game.

Good Social Media Manager's will create and source relevant content and this takes time. Creating content can involve making images with text or where social media is growing more visual it can be creating videos. Some bloggers take courses in social media management before launching themselves on clients. Donna Billson from LittleLilyPad has made the transition and has many clients we asked her just how she goes about finding clients.

The best way to secure new clients is through recommendation but social media is all about social and so you need to be networking to find them. Whether it is being present on LinkedIn or sites such as People Per Hour or physically going to networking events, companies especially SME's want to deal with a real person rather than a faceless corporation.

How much time is spent on each client depends on the frequency of posting. A basic package often starts at two hours a week and this would include creating content for Facebook and Twitter and posting each day on the platform. The second part is responding to comments and speaking for the client. Many smaller businesses will employ someone to do their social media as they recognise how important it is to have a voice online yet they may not have the time, interest or skills to run the channels. Rates for social media vary on experience but it can be from £15 to £30 per hour. To find this type of work look on freelance sites including Upwork, Elance and People Per Hour but like many things, directly approaching small companies that you have built a relationship up with is a possible way too. Attending local networking lunches may open doors and is another reason networking is a vital tool.

Blog Design

Blog Design and troubleshooting is another viable income stream for bloggers who have the technical skills. In our experience bloggers who can offer this service are often kept busy with work. Emma always pays for technical support and blog redesigns as it is not an area she is confident in and when things go wrong she wants them fixed fast!

Some bloggers also like having new themes or headers on a regular basis and if you can provide these services you will be in demand. Bloggers that offer this service charge can charge on an hourly rate or they may have a fixed rate for services. An hourly rate can be from £20 per hour with a complete blog design costing between £100-£500. Hannah Fleming from Hi Baby Blog offers WordPress support and has been a valuable asset providing technical support to get **www.bloggingyourwaytoriches.com** up and running.

Copy writing and Editing

Copywriting and editing are also a highly saleable skill. There are plenty of sites where freelancers can sell their copywriting skills or bid for work. This is often lower paid work and the rates vary immensely. Many bloggers initially expect the pay to be similar to sponsored posts but this is not the case. When paying for a sponsored post the client is not just paying for the words you write but access to your audience, the readers you have built up over months and years. With copywriting, the client is just paying for your words and the rates reflect this.

When writing for others you may charge an hourly rate and again anything from £10 upwards is normal. If you are looking for work sites like People Per Hour are a good starting point. There are many opportunities listed daily and you pitch for the work. It is free to pitch for work and can be another good way to grow your skill set and gain contacts. The work on offer may involve writing blogs for other companies and this can give you experience of writing for others and often the work requires little research. However, if you do need to read up on a topic do factor that time into your rates.

E-Courses

A small number of experienced bloggers have also developed e-courses or training programmes where they share what they have learnt over the years. They charge others to enrol on their e-courses in which they share the secrets their success and explain to newer bloggers how to build a successful career from blogging. These courses may focus on specific skills and benefit bloggers.

E-Books

Kindle e-books are another way that bloggers can diversify and make money as a spin off from their blog. E-books can contain affiliate links which means that the author makes money when readers click on the links and the links lead to sales. Other bloggers sell their e-books which may or may not be on a topic close to their blog.

Becky Goddard Hill from Family Budgeting gives this advice on diversifying your income:

There are so many opportunities that arise form blogging and diversifying keeps the work fresh and fun. I have made money writing eBooks, speaking at conferences being a resident blogger on a brand websites and taking part in consultancy work for brands wanting to expand their social media.

We end this chapter with the methods Emma and Lynn are using to diversify. They realised over time that lots of bloggers were contacting them about how to blog, how to negotiate fees, and how to pitch to brands. When enough people approached them asking the same questions it clicked that they were the experts in these fields and could explore projects to generate income.

Many bloggers blog about blogging and earn affiliate revenue from for example recommending blog hosting companies. A few have recently started online blogging courses. Emma and Lynn decided to write this book.

The thought behind Blogging Your Way To Riches is that it is cost effective handbook that provides the information required for blogging success. Expertise and experiences could be shared in a book and the reality of blogging with all its highs and lows. Readers can pick it up when they want and read whatever suits their agenda and dip into chapters time and time again.

We hope that this chapter has inspired you to look outside your blog and consider it as a springboard for other opportunities. Blogging can be just the start of a portfolio career where you have multiple income streams and the ability to make life changing amounts of money. Couple the income derived from the blog and opportunities off the blog and this is where bloggers can start generating a large income.

+

Chapter 18 - Conclusion

Blogging Your Way To Riches was written to provide answers to the big questions about blogging, from how your blog should look, to how to monetise your blog, to the guidelines you should follow and the networking needed to bring success.

Both Emma and Lynn wanted to share what they have learnt in the past few years after leaving their previous careers to forge their own businesses online.

They wanted to demonstrate that blogging is now a viable option for people looking to create a new career. Blogging can be a career that puts you in control of your future, a career where you get to be creative, to write, to take photographs and to earn money doing what you love. To build a successful blog takes time, determination and organisation but, the rewards can be worth the effort.

Blogging has exploded in recent years and as more and more brands turn their attention to us, the digital influencers, who knows what the future holds. One thing is certain, bloggers and blogging are here to stay. More and more blogs are being started every day and as an industry we are becoming a powerful tool for advertising and marketing. The future looks good as we find new, exciting and engaging ways of working with brands and sharing our opinions with our growing audiences.

Emma and Lynn hope that Blogging Your Way To Riches has inspired you to start or continue on your personal blogging journey. There is plenty more room for bloggers to bring their skills and experiences to an ever-growing audience. Whether you write about parenting, finance, food, interiors or any other niche, blogging can bring you everything you dream about.

Emma and Lynn changed their lives for the better, after taking the risk of becoming self-employed and have shown that it can be done.

Now it is your turn. Where would you like blogging to take you?

Glossary

There are many technical terms in this book that might be new to some bloggers. Here is a handy glossary to explain the terms we use in the book.

Search Engine Optimisation

Search engine optimisation (SEO) is the process of affecting the visibility of a website or a web page in a web search engine's unpaid results—often referred to as "natural" or "organic" search results. SEO is most closely associated with Google the most popular search engine of choice. Think of Google as the ultimate dictionary or index for content on the internet. There is a hugely complex mathematical algorithm that sits behind it which changes the order of websites appearing for search terms constantly.

Search Term

These are the words that internet users type into a search engine when looking for content. These will be the key words that you include in the SEO settings of your blog post.

Follow link/ No-follow link

This refers to website links you include on your blog posts. In an unpaid natural post, you may include links to other websites these will be direct follow links that point traffic towards that site. The other site will get Google Juice (helps Google natural ranking) from these links. A no-follow link should be used in sponsored posts, the no-follow refers to coding you place around the web site address and the recipient website will not get any Google juice from the link.

It is against Google guidelines to include a follow link to a company who has paid for a sponsored post.

Domain Authority

This is trust rating of your website and is a number from 1 to 100. A DA score is only reliable if the blog is self-hosted or has a vanity URL. Blogspot and wordpress.com addresses do not have their own DA score. You can check yours on the MOZ website. The BBC is 100, a most trusted website. Some brand will only work with sites with DA of at least 20 or 25. 25 is a great score to aim for.

It can be increased by including lot of great original content, natural follow links from other websites and time, the longer a website has existed the higher its DA will be.

Guest post

This is a post written by a guest writer on your blog, this may be another blogger or a friend or a paid contributor. You can also write guest posts for others. There is often a reciprocal agreement between bloggers with a guest post for guest post. This helps with domain authority.

Affiliate income/links

You are an affiliate when you promote products for a brand and are paid a commission for every sale that the brand makes via the customer that bought via your website. It can all be tracked via affiliate links.

Facebook share/Re-Tweet

These are broadly the same. A post can be reposted from your Facebook or Twitter account to another page. This helps to get more and more traffic to your site

Google Analytics

A tool to set up on your website and gives you all the statistics you need for insight to your website. Including post traffic, where traffic has come from, social media sources of traffic, google sources all over many periods of time.

Unique Monthly Users

A statistic often quoted as traffic which can be found from Google. The number of unique visitors to your website. One person visiting every week in a month will be counted once.

Page Views

This number will be bigger than the unique monthly users and is the number of pages viewed in total from all your users.

Bounce Rate

This is a % meaning the number of people who leave your website after reading a page. The aim is to get this rate as low as possible with people jumping from page to page within your site rather than jumping off to another site.

Self-hosted website

This is a website where you pay a company to host your website and you have a URL such as **www.mrsmummypenny.co.uk** rather than a blogger or WordPress URL. Most brands will only work with self-hosted bloggers.

Header

This is the graphic at the top of your website that states your blog name. It should also be replicated across social media. This should look professional and will represent your brand.

Blog demographic

These are the types of people that read your website and visit your social media pages. Age range, sex, location. Your insights can be gleaned from Google Analytics and Social Media Insights.

Vlog

This is a video blog normally hosted on YouTube

Back links

This is where another website links to yours. It gives great Google Juice helping you to get more traffic and helps with your domain authority.

Linky

This is themed post hosted by a blogger or group if bloggers. Other blogger add links from their relevant posts to this linky. Other bloggers will read and comment on your post and you should read as many posts as possible and comment on their blog post too.

Media Pack

A pack of information on your blog to send to PR agencies. It should contain an introduction to you, your social media statistics, blog traffic, how to work with you, a brand page with previous campaigns, demographics and your prices

Contact Us

Emma Bradley and Lynn James can be contacted at **press@bloggingyourwaytoriches.com** and on their website **www.bloggingyourwaytoriches.com**

Or via their social media channels.

Emma:

www.Emmaand3.com

www.MumsSavvySavings.com

twitter.com/emmaand3

www.facebook.com/Emmaand3

www.instagram.com/emmaand3

\+

www.linkedin.com/in/emma-bradley

www.youtube.com/user/emmaand3

Lynn:

www.mrsmummypenny.co.uk

twitter.com/MrsMummypennyUK

www.facebook.com/MrsMummypenny

www.instagram.com/mrsmummypennyuk/

www.linkedin.com/in/lynn-james

64130257R00107

Made in the USA
Charleston, SC
26 November 2016